Destination Bethlehem

Seven Christmas Plays for Young People

Steve Trott

A Division of Baker Book House Co
Grand Rapids, Michigan 49516

Dedicated to Rev. Howard Vande Guchte,
who first opened doors

©1993 by Steve Trott

Published by Baker Books
a division of Baker Book House Company
P.O. Box 6287, Grand Rapids, Michigan 49516-6287

Printed in the United States of America

For individual church use, plays may be copied—one for each member of the production—without fee. For all other uses, all rights are reserved. No part of this publication may be reproduced, stored in a retrieval system, or transmitted in any form or by any means—electronic, mechanical, photocopy, recording, or any other—without the prior written permission of the publisher. The only exception is brief quotations in printed reviews.

Library of Congress Cataloging-in-Publication Data

Trott, Steve.
     Destination Bethlehem : seven Christmas plays for young people / Steve Trott.
        p.   cm.
     Contents: Buster come back—Destination Bethlehem—Did I miss anything important?—R.S.V.P.—Something sacred this way comes—Nocturne—You don't say!
     ISBN 0-8010-8906-9
     1. Children's plays, American. 2. Christmas plays, American. [1. Christmas—Drama. 2. Plays.] I. Title.
PS3570.R593D47   1993
812'.54—dc20   93-19352

Scripture quotations are from the HOLY BIBLE, NEW INTERNATIONAL VERSION®. NIV®. Copyright © 1973, 1978, 1984 by International Bible Society. Used by permission of Zondervan Publishing House. All rights reserved.

Verses marked LB are taken from *The Living Bible*, copyright © 1971 by Tyndale House Publishers, Wheaton, Illinois. Used by permission.

Verses marked NASB are from the New American Standard Bible, © the Lockman Foundation 1960, 1962, 1963, 1968, 1971, 1972, 1973, 1975, 1977.

Verses marked KJV are from the King James Version.

Contents

Introduction   5
Buster Come Back   7
Destination Bethlehem   17
Did I Miss Anything Important?   27
R.S.V.P.   37
Something Sacred This Way Comes   42
Nocturne   46
You Don't Say!   54
Appendix: Music Sources   63

Introduction

From the days when Santa Claus was the central figure of my Christmases, I have within the scrapbook of my memory the recollection of a certain gift that somehow went undiscovered until halfway to Epiphany. Apparently, amid the claim-staking chaos of Christmas Eve, this particular prize had been inadvertently demoted from its place of honor beneath O Tannenbaum to a downhill (and less dignified) position underneath an upholstered chair.

In actuality, the mail-order purchase had arrived several days after Santa's scheduled appearance, necessitating the creative subterfuge by those in the know: a plot that those of us who were not in the know readily swallowed—hook, pine, and tinsel. (After all, if you're gullible enough to believe that reindeer can fly, or better yet, that Santa can find that many house numbers in the dark—and without headlights—you're liable to believe anything, including stories about gifts getting shoved off piles and under chairs only to be discovered days later while Mom is vacuuming. Besides, at Christmas what counts is the bottom line: Although I was none the wiser, I was one gift richer.)

None of which has anything to do with the present collection. Except this: There is only one gift that really matters at Christmas—the gift of eternal life that God has provided through Jesus Christ. It is a gift that has, on more than one occasion, found itself unnoticed, unopened, and unclaimed, lost beneath the discarded wrappings and trappings of a high-tech hectic holiday—hidden under the upholstery, if you will, until halfway to eternity.

I heard it said recently that one of the problems in presenting the Good News to people is that it's no longer news to many of them. Like those stagnant oft-repeated ads we so easily ignore, the rich benevolence of the Christmas story can easily be relegated to the status of a well-acquainted commercial, if not presented in new, refreshing, and insightful ways. It has been my goal in creating the following productions to provide church and school groups of all ages with creative, nontraditional Christmas programs that will stimulate the hearts and imaginations of those doing the presenting, while capturing the attention of those receiving the gift.

Buster Come Back

> The last thing we do is to come.
> Oswald Chambers
> *My Utmost for His Highest*

Subject
God is calling—will we come?

Setting
A front porch in mid-December.

Summary

1. A boy searches for his dog, Buster.
2. Young neighborhood children spell out the program theme with snowmen.
3. Older neighborhood children happen by on their way to toboggan hills and home from shopping. They read Bible verses illustrating mankind's reluctance to respond to God's persistent calling.
4. Solo: returning to God is compared to falling snow.
5. A group of runaway canines discusses the pros and cons of freedom.
6. Carolers gather on the porch to sing the Christmas story. During the songs, a living manger scene is created on the front lawn.
7. Buster comes home.
8. All of the children gather around the manger scene for final songs.
9. Solo: God is calling us to come to Jesus.

Characters

BRANDON, *a boy minus Buster*
MELISSA, *his older sister*
FATHER, *could be played by adult or high-school student*
MOTHER, *could be played by adult or high-school student*
CHILDREN, *twelve or more for building snowmen*
READERS, *fifteen; or cut lines for fewer readers*
CAROLERS, *as many as you wish; at least six*
SOLOIST, *male or female*
BUSTER, *a dog; male*
FIDO, *a dog; male or female*
SPOT, *a dog; male or female*
OPHELIA, *a dog; female*
PAVLOV, *a dog; male*
Other dogs with no lines if desired

Nativity scene (lawn statues):

MARY
JOSEPH
ANGELS, *optional; any number*
SHEPHERDS, *optional; any number*

Destination Bethlehem

It is night, so the stage is dark.

A flashlight enters, attached to the hand of a young boy, Brandon. After pointing the beam of light in several directions, including a few sweeps across the audience, the boy calls out anxiously.

BRANDON Bus-ter! Bus-ter! *(pause, then louder, almost angry)* Buster!

He sits down, dejected, center stage, and turns off the flashlight. After a few moments a porch light comes on above him. In its glow we can see that Brandon is sitting on the steps of a front porch. It is his own house, and in a moment his sister Melissa opens the door behind him and pokes her head out.

MELISSA Brandon?

His only reply is a slight raising of his hand in a sort of half wave. Melissa steps outside and, after her next line, sits down beside her brother.

MELISSA Buster's run off again?

BRANDON Stupid dog.

MELISSA He's not stupid. He's just—curious. He loves having his freedom.

BRANDON He doesn't realize the danger.

MELISSA He'll be okay. Don't worry.

BRANDON Easy for you to say.

MELISSA Yeah, you're right. If he was my dog I'd be a nervous wreck.

BRANDON It's just not very easy being a parent.

MELISSA *(amused)* Parent! He's your dog, not your kid!

BRANDON Well I *feel* like a parent. I worry about him. Yesterday I'm taking him for his walk and he sees a squirrel—across the street, up on a branch—I mean, what's he gonna do, climb the stupid tree? He takes off, racing. If I hadn't had a tight grip on his leash he woulda run right in front of a snowplow!

MELISSA You really love that mutt, don't you.

BRANDON He's not a mutt.

MELISSA That's not the point.

BRANDON I care about what happens to him, that's all.

MELISSA You love him.

BRANDON I just don't want him to come home smelling like a skunk again.

MELISSA You love him.

BRANDON Why won't he learn to come when I call? What does he think I'm gonna *do* to him, anyway?

MELISSA He doesn't know any better.

BRANDON	But he knows I love— *(catches himself)*
MELISSA	Say it: You love him.
BRANDON	*(upset)* Why won't he come when I call!

He rises and begins calling out Buster's name again as he exits to continue his search. Melissa rises and follows close behind him. After a few seconds the tree lights come on in the window. Immediately Mother and Father come out the front door and stand on the porch to address the audience.

MOTHER	*(quoting Brandon)* Why won't he come when I call? That's a question God has probably asked himself over and over again: Why won't my people come when I call?
FATHER	You know, he's been calling for a long time. It began back in the book of Genesis when Adam and Eve decided to disobey God *(quotes Genesis 3:8–9 from NIV Bible)*.

> Then the man and his wife
> heard the sound of the Lord God
> as he was walking in the garden
> in the cool of the day,
> and they hid from the Lord God
> among the trees of the garden.
> But the Lord God called to the man,
> "Where are you?"

MOTHER	From that point on, the story of Scripture is the story of God's invitation to people everywhere to come out of hiding and return to him. And that's also the theme of tonight's program. I've asked some of the neighborhood children to help us illustrate that message by building some snowmen in our front yard.
FATHER	Snowmen? To illustrate a message?
MOTHER	Yes. Perhaps you'd like to help them. Here they come now.

Instrumental version of Frosty the Snowman *is performed in the background as a company of at least nine of your program's youngest children enter, carrying or rolling nine large white discs or spheres. These come in the three sizes typical of actual snowmen—head, torso, and base—and on each is painted a large black letter, either O, M, or E. Three snowmen are quickly constructed either in front of the porch or off to one side, depending on the amount of space available. When finished, the far-right figure will consist of three snowballs bearing the letter E, the center figure the letter M, and the figure on the left the letter O. Brooms, scarves, hats, and other traditional accessories may be added as long as they don't block the letters, which at this point spell nothing of consequence. Mother and Father take note of this fact as they stand facing the snowmen, unaware that behind them, another snowman is approaching from stage right. Already built, it is being delivered via plastic sled, pulled and guided by several more young children.*

FATHER	Well, they look great, but I'm not sure what they have to do with the theme of the program.
MOTHER	Yes, something is definitely missing. Does anyone have any idea what it could be?

CHILDREN	Over there!

They are pointing toward the fourth snowman, the head of which bears the letter C, the torso the letter H, and the base the letter T. When it is stationed next to the other three snowmen, the words COME HOME TO ME take form. The children applaud.

MOTHER	Very good!
FATHER	Now I get it!
MOTHER	Would somebody like to read the message so that everyone can hear it? *(chooses a child)*
CHILD 1	Come home to me.
MOTHER	Yes—and can someone tell me what that means? Come home to me? *(chooses another child)*
CHILD 2	It means God is inviting us to come home to him.
MOTHER	Yes, that's right. And it's an important message, especially at Christmastime, isn't it. *(they nod)* Now I'm wondering if any of you would like to come into *my* home for a nice hot cup of cocoa.
CHILDREN	Me! Me! I would! *(etc.)*
MOTHER	Well okay, then, into the kitchen!

Children follow her through the front door. As they exit, Reader 1 enters from side, quietly shoveling the sidewalk next door. Someone, perhaps one of your young people, begins playing O Come, O Come, Emmanuel *softly on the piano; it continues under all the readings but must not drown them out.*

FATHER	Hi Jim! *(or* Jamie, *if a girl)*
READER 1	Hi Mr. *(insert name)*!
FATHER	Still earning money towards college, I see.
READER 1	Uh-huh. Another winter like last year and I'll be able to go to Harvard!
FATHER	That's for sure! How do you like our snowmen?
READER 1	Not too bad! *(continues shoveling)*
FATHER	*(to audience)* You know, over the years God has sent a few snowmen himself bearing that same message. *(indicates snowmen)* They were called prophets. And their job, among other things, was to remind mankind that God wants us to remain close to him. Perhaps the prophet who said it best was Hosea, who shared these thoughts from God about the people of Israel.

Reader 1 lifts shovel and reads from a page taped to the metal the following Living Bible translation of Hosea 11:1–5, 8. The passage can be divided among two or three shovelers if necessary.

READER 1	When Israel was a child I loved him as a son And brought him out of Egypt. But the more I called to him, the more he rebelled . . . I trained him from infancy, I taught him to walk, I held him in my arms. But he doesn't know or even care that it was I who raised him. As a man would lead his favorite ox, so I led Israel with my ropes of love. I loosened his muzzle so he could eat. I myself have stooped and fed him. But my people shall return to Egypt . . . because they won't return to me . . . Oh, how can I give you up . . . How can I let you go? . . . My heart cries out within me; how I long to help you!

A host of neighbor children begin passing by on their way to or from various wintertime activities. You may wish for all to enter at once; otherwise bring them in according to the stage directions that follow. Readers 2 through 5 enter carrying sleds and saucers. Cards taped to the top sides contain verses from the Living Bible, Jeremiah 7:22–26.

FATHER	The prophet Jeremiah had a few things to say on this subject as well. Listen to these words from God to his people.
READER 2	It wasn't offerings and sacrifices I wanted from your fathers when I led them out of Egypt. That was not the point of my command.
READER 3	But what I told them was: *Obey* me and I will be your God and you shall be my people; only do as I say and all shall be well!
READER 4	But they wouldn't listen; they kept on doing whatever they wanted to, following their own stubborn, evil thoughts. They went backward instead of forward.
READER 5	Ever since the day your fathers left Egypt until now, I have kept on sending them my prophets, day after day. But they wouldn't listen to them or even try to hear.

Destination Bethlehem

Readers 6 through 8 enter carrying a toboggan. They read from verses taped to the pad: the Living Bible translation of Jeremiah 8:4–7.

READER 6 — Once again give them this message from the Lord:
When a person falls, he jumps up again;
when he is on the wrong road
and discovers his mistake,
he goes back to the fork
where he made the wrong turn.
But these people keep on along their evil path,
even though I warn them.

READER 7 — I listen to their conversation and what do I hear?
Is anyone sorry for sin?
Does anyone say, "What a terrible thing I have done?"
No, all are rushing pell-mell down the path of sin
as swiftly as a horse rushing to the battle!

READER 8 — The stork knows the time of her migration,
as does the turtledove, and the crane, and the swallow.
They all return at God's appointed time each year;
but not my people!

Two hockey players enter, dressed in full uniforms if available. They carry hockey sticks and have their skates hanging around their necks. Or perhaps they wear roller blades and actually skate on and off the stage. They can read their verses from 3" x 5" cards taped into their hockey gloves, or you may want them to be dressed as goalies wearing masks: Reader 9 takes off his mask and reads, from a card taped inside, the NIV translation of Psalm 32:8–9; then Reader 10 takes off her mask and reads the Living Bible translation of Ezekiel 34:11–12, 16.

FATHER — King David and the prophet Ezekiel also spoke of the Lord's invitation for us to come to him.

READER 9 — I will instruct you and teach you
in the way you should go;
I will counsel you and watch over you.
Do not be like the horse or the mule,
which have no understanding
but must be controlled by bit and bridle
or they will not come to you.

READER 10 — For the Lord God says:
I will search and find my sheep.
I will be like a shepherd
looking for his flock.
I will find my sheep and rescue them
from all the places they were scattered . . .
I will seek my lost ones,
those who strayed away,
and bring them safely home again.

Mother comes back out onto the porch as Readers 11 through 15 enter carrying gift-wrapped packages home from shopping. They will share verses taped to the boxes: the NIV translation of Isaiah 55:1–3, 6–7, and 1:18.

FATHER The prophet Isaiah is popular at Christmastime because of his predictions about the coming of the Messiah. But he also wrote some very important words on the subject of repentance—which is part of what coming to God is all about. Listen to these Christmas gifts from the book of Isaiah.

READER 11 Come, all you who are thirsty,
come to the waters;
and you who have no money,
come, buy and eat!

READER 12 Listen, listen to me,
and eat what is good . . .
Give ear and come to me;
hear me, that your soul may live.

READER 13 Seek the Lord
while he may be found;
call on him
while he is near.

READER 14 Let the wicked forsake his way
and the evil man his thoughts.
Let him turn to the Lord,
and he will have mercy on him,
and to our God,
for he will freely pardon.

READER 15 "Come now, let us reason together,"
says the Lord. "Though your sins
are like scarlet, they shall be
as white as snow."

MOTHER (*sings* Somewhere It's Snowing *by Stephanie Boosahda*)

As she sings she walks among the children, addressing the words to them. If you have the equipment, this scene would be effective using a spotlight and falling snow. At the conclusion of the song the lights fade out and all exit. In the ensuing darkness, after an appropriate pause for impact, the sound of a dog barking is heard from the back of the auditorium. He is answered by another dog from off to one side. A third from yet another direction joins in, and then a fourth. Lights come up as these four gather, either off to one side of the stage or at the front of the center aisle; they should not be perceived as being anywhere near the front porch but rather off somewhere in the distance. The dogs sniff at each other in greeting. After a few moments of this, Buster comes running to join them, barking all the way.

OTHERS Buster! Hey Buster! Buster, how ya doing? (*etc.*)

More sniffing all around.

PAVLOV	Freedom! *(all howl)*
OPHELIA	No more fences! *(all howl)*
BUSTER	No more leashes! *(all howl)*
FIDO	Nobody saying to me: Fido, stop that barking!
SPOT	*(making fun)* Fido? What kind of a name is *that*?
FIDO	It's a *dog's* name. What did you expect?
SPOT	Not very creative, if you ask me.
FIDO	So what's *your* name?
SPOT	*(hesitates, embarrassed)* Spot.
FIDO	*Spot! (sarcastic)* Wow! That's original!
	Others laugh: Ar! Ar! Ar! Ar!
SPOT	Who needs names anyway? They're just one more way for our owners to try to control us.
OPHELIA	Yeah. They think just because they yell our names out, we should come running. Well, we've got *better* things to do!
BUSTER	Yeah. *(pause as he reflects)* Like what?
OPHELIA	*(thinking)* Well—like sniffing, for instance.
OTHERS	Sniffing! Yeah! *(etc.) (they sniff)*
PAVLOV	So many smells and so little time!
SPOT	Oh boy! This freedom's gonna be so great!
BUSTER	Yeah. Doin' whatever we wanna do, whenever we feel like it.
OPHELIA	*(yawns)* Sleeping beneath the moon—
FIDO	*Barking* at the moon! *(a bit of barking by all)*
OPHELIA	It'll be perfect. *(lies down)* Well, almost perfect. This cold, hard ground's gonna take some getting used to after all those years of sleeping on the carpet.
SPOT	Carpet? You slept on the carpet?
OPHELIA	*(proud of it; she thinks Spot is impressed)* Yeah—the carpet.
SPOT	*(not impressed)* Ha! She had to sleep on the floor!
OPHELIA	*(defensive)* Carpet. I said *carpet*. There's a difference.
SPOT	*(bragging) I* slept on a *blanket* on *top* of the carpet.
FIDO	*(looking down his muzzle)* Blanket? Pfff! *I* had my own *dog bed*.
PAVLOV	Dog beds are for the underprivileged. I slept on top of Kathy's bed!
OPHELIA	*(impressed)* On the *bed?* You're kidding!

PAVLOV	No—I'm not. Of course, sometimes her feet are in the way, and once in a while she'll forget I'm there and throw the blanket over me. *(sighs)* But—privilege has its price, that's what *I* always say.
BUSTER	You guys are pathetic.
PAVLOV	Wha—?
FIDO	How do you figure?
BUSTER	*(bragging) My* master lets me sleep right under the covers *with* him. Or—at least he *used* to—back in the days when I *allowed* myself beneath his authority.
BRANDON	*(calling from offstage)* Bus-ter! Time for sup-per!
BUSTER	*(perking up)* Supper? *Supper?*

He's gone—barking all the way. The others follow on his heels, exiting in the direction of the voice—and the food. Lights fade out.

CAROLERS	*(sing* Here We Come A-Caroling*)*

From offstage a group of carolers is heard approaching. As lights come up again they enter from down the street, then make their way to the front steps where they finish the song. Father and Mother appear at the door and, at the conclusion, step outside.

FATHER	God's *greatest* invitation for us to come to him was in coming himself to us. When Jesus was born in Bethlehem, it was part of God's plan to provide a means by which we could be with him forever. It was his way of calling each of us home.
CAROLERS	*(sing* The Virgin Mary Had a Baby Boy*)*

Mary—carrying the baby Jesus—and Joseph enter during the song and take positions on the lawn in front of the porch, creating an outdoor nativity scene. If you wish to add angels and shepherds, bring them in at the appropriate moments during this song. Following the music, Mother and Father will quote from the NIV translation of Matthew 11:28 and 19:14.

MOTHER	This baby born in Bethlehem would one day grow up to speak these words to all who would listen:
FATHER	Come to me, all you who are weary and burdened, and I will give you rest.
MOTHER	And these words: Let the little children come to me, and do not hinder them, for the kingdom of heaven belongs to such as these.
CAROLERS	*(sing* O Come, Little Children*)*

During the song, the children who built the snowmen enter and gather around the nativity scene. Father will quote from the NIV translation of Luke 19:10.

MOTHER	Finally Jesus would speak these words about his purpose for coming to earth:

Destination Bethlehem

FATHER
: For the Son of Man came
to seek and to save what was lost.

CAROLERS
: (*sing* Bring a Torch, Jeanette, Isabella)

> *The lights fade as the music begins and from entrances throughout the auditorium all of the readers enter carrying flashlights. They sweep beams of light across the audience, the walls, and the ceiling as they make their way to the front, eventually joining the others around the nativity scene. As the song ends the lights come up again, and Brandon enters, carrying a small dog—either an actual puppy or a life-sized stuffed toy.*

BRANDON
: Hey, everybody! Buster came back!

> *Everyone cheers as Brandon makes his way to the porch, accompanied by Melissa. As the introduction to the next song is heard, all of the dogs enter and sit down in front of the nativity scene.*

EVERYONE
: (*sings* Rise, Come and See the King)

PASTOR
: (*could speak a few words at this point*)

SOLOIST
: (*sings* The Word *by Michael Card*)

(*alternate selection:* Immanuel *by Michael Card, or* Turn Your Heart toward Home *by the Chapmans*)

Destination Bethlehem

> Were we led all that way for
> Birth or Death?
>
> T. S. Eliot
> *Journey of the Magi*

Subject

Journeying to Bethlehem—and to God.

Setting

A car, a chorus, and empty space.

Summary

1. A family of five sets out for Grandma's.
2. To help the children pass the time along the way, the father offers a riddle: What are the four famous journeys made on the occasion of the first Christmas?
3. One of the children in the car identifies the first journey: Mary and Joseph traveling to Bethlehem for the census.
4. A second child identifies the second journey: the shepherds coming into the city after hearing the announcement made by the angels.
5. The third child identifies the third journey: the magi's expedition from the East.
6. Mother identifies the fourth journey: the Son of God coming down from heaven to be born in a manger.
7. Mother then suggests that there is a fifth journey.
8. Father guesses (and almost drives off the road): the journey each of us must make in coming to Christ.
9. After each answer is discovered, an appropriate Bible passage and corresponding Christmas song are heard on the car radio (children's chorus) and a reenactment of the scene is presented.

Characters

FATHER, *can be played by an older child or adult*
MOTHER, *can be played by an older child or adult*
GARRY, *the oldest child; a boy*
SHERI, *the middle child; a girl*
TERRY, *the youngest child; a girl or boy*
SINGER, *preferably male; a hitchhiker*
GRANDMA, *optional; brief, silent appearance at end*
SHEPHERDS, *as many as ten; male or female*
WISE MEN, *three or more*
CARAVAN, *optional; any number*
ANGEL, *male or female, possibly a dancer*
MARY
JOSEPH
CHORUS, *any number; singing and sound effects*
READERS, *as many as desired; read selections from Scripture; also two radio announcers*

Destination Bethlehem

On the right stands a chorus of children. On the left, a car. Actually, the car looks more like a couple of benches or two short rows of chairs, but the audience will get the idea. Father enters from right and crosses to car, stopping for a moment on the way to check his watch and to motion impatiently behind him.

FATHER — Come on, you guys! We're gonna be late!

He opens imaginary car door and sits in driver's seat. As he mimes turning key in ignition, chorus imitates car engine failing to start.

CHORUS — Oonder-reeer-reeer-reeer-reeer.

He stops, pumps imaginary gas pedal, then turns key again.

CHORUS — Oonder-reeer-reeer-reeer-reeer.

He stops, frowns, pumps again, turns key.

CHORUS — Oonder-reeer-reeer-reeer-reeer-reeer-reeer-reeeeer.

Father gets out, mimes lifting hood, then stands there, hands on hips, pondering the problem. After a moment he takes from the trunk or from his coat pocket a huge, oversized tool, perhaps a wrench or screwdriver, and ever so lightly taps a portion of the imaginary engine.

CHORUS — (quietly) Ping!

He gives a satisfied nod, closes the hood, gets back in the car, and turns key once again.

CHORUS — Verrrooooooommm!

He smiles and sighs contentedly. After a moment he looks at his watch again, realizes how late it's getting, and presses imaginary horn.

CHORUS — Beeep beeeep!

FATHER — Hurry up, you guys! Grandma will be wondering what happened to us!

Mother and three young children file out, carrying an assortment of items: toys, dolls, sports equipment, games, books, pumpkin pie, loaf of bread—whatever a family with children might take to Grandma's on Christmas. Father puts most of these things in the trunk (out of sight behind the back row of chairs). Finally all are seated in the car, ready to leave: Garry, the oldest, sitting behind Mother; Terry, the youngest, sitting behind Father; and Sheri, the middle child, sitting in the middle. Suddenly Mother and Father look at each other; she puts a hand to her mouth, his own drops open. He exits quickly, then returns carrying a car seat, which he places in the front seat between them. As Mother tends briefly to the imaginary baby in the car seat, Father begins driving, holding a real or imaginary steering wheel in his hands and rotating it occasionally to simulate left and right turns.

MOTHER — Well—should we see if we can find some nice Christmas music on the radio?

OTHERS — Yeah!

She reaches for an imaginary knob and mimes turning radio on.

CHORUS — (One or more members of the chorus sing a line or two of a currently popular non-Christmas song that the audience will recognize and chuckle over.)

MOTHER	*(turning knob)* That's definitely *not* what I was looking for!

> *Garry is disappointed as Mother selects another station, but lights up again as he recognizes a pro football broadcast.*

READER	*(as announcer)* And so, with only three minutes left in the first half, Buffalo has finally moved into Dolphin territory.
SHERI	What are buffaloes doing in the ocean?
GARRY	Not that kind of buffaloes! The Buffalo Bills!
SHERI	*(perplexed)* I know *ducks* have bills, but I never heard of a *buffalo* having a bill.

> *Garry rolls his eyes and shakes his head, then turns to look out imaginary window. Mother is by now continuing her search for Christmas music.*

SHERI	Ducks would have a lot better chance out there in the ocean with the dolphins than *buffaloes* would, *that's* for sure.

> *Garry groans. Mother has found a new station—right in the middle of an opera broadcast. A soprano is hitting a high note at the moment.*

CHORUS	*(a soloist)* Aaaaaaahhhh—
FAMILY	*(covering their ears)* Nooooo!

> *Mother quickly changes station.*

READER	*(as radio announcer)* And now, let's get back to some more Christmas music, shall we?
MOTHER	*Here* we go—
READER	*(as radio announcer)* I'm sure you'll enjoy this next selection sung by *(name of church, name of chorus)*.
CHORUS	*(sings* Over the River and through the Woods*)*

> *As the chorus performs, the family joins in. During the song Father occasionally turns the steering wheel to the right or left; as he does so, everyone in the car leans in one direction or the other. They might also, as a unit, rise a bit and then sink down again to simulate the car going over a hill. Following the song, you may wish your younger chorus members to exit. If so, allow them to leave before the dialogue resumes.*

GARRY	Are we there yet?
TERRY	Are we there yet?

> *Terry has stuck her head right next to her father's left ear. She stays there for her next two lines.*

SHERI	How much farther?
TERRY	How much farther?
GARRY	I'm hungry!
SHERI	I'm thirsty!

Destination Bethlehem

TERRY	I think I'm going to be sick!

Father reaches up with his right hand and pulls Terry's stocking cap down over her face. She sits back down.

FATHER	Okay, listen everybody. I've got something to help make the trip go quicker.
GARRY	What?
SHERI	A game?
FATHER	A riddle. Here it is: Who can tell me the four journeys that were made on the first Christmas?
GARRY	Huh?
TERRY	Huh?
SHERI	You're difficult to understand, Dad.
FATHER	There were four famous journeys that people made to Bethlehem on the first Christmas. Can you tell me who made those journeys? Take them one at a time.

Garry jumps up and excitedly reaches across the front seat to grab his dad by the shoulder, practically pulling him over. Father struggles to maintain control of the car.

GARRY	I know! I know! I got the first one!
FATHER	*(regaining control)* Okay. Okay. What's the first one?
GARRY	The first journey to Bethlehem was—Mary and Joseph going there and finding no room in the inn.
FATHER	Exactly! Yes, and can anyone remember why they had to go to Bethlehem in the first place? *(pause)* Nobody?
MOTHER	I'll give you a hint: Caesar's—
GARRY	*(excited)* Caesar's pizza! *(they laugh)*
TERRY	Pizza pizza.
GARRY	I mean—not pizza—Caesar's census.
MOTHER	That's right. They went for Caesar's census.

Lights fade on car as one or more members of the choir read from the NIV translation of Luke 2:1–7.

READER	In those days Caesar Augustus issued a decree that a census should be taken of the entire Roman world . . . And everyone went to his own town to register.
READER	So Joseph also went up from the town of Nazareth in Galilee . . . to Bethlehem the town of David, because he belonged to the house and line of David.

READER	He went there to register with Mary, who was pledged to be married to him and was expecting a child. While they were there, the time came for the baby to be born, and she gave birth to her firstborn, a son.
READER	She wrapped him in strips of cloth and placed him in a manger, because there was no room for them in the inn.
CHORUS	(*sings* O Little Town of Bethlehem)

> *As the chorus sings, Mary and Joseph enter, either down an aisle or from left of the chorus. They stop and form the beginning elements of a manger scene: either right in front of the chorus or in between the chorus and the car, depending on the size of your stage. Joseph is carrying a couple of blankets and places one of these in a feeding trough that he finds nearby. Although there is as yet no baby in it, the manger scene is assembled as though there were. At the end of the song, Mary and Joseph hold their positions and lights come up again on the family in the car.*

FATHER	Well, that song on the radio fits in pretty well. Let's see if we can come up with another answer before the next song begins. Who can tell me the second journey to Bethlehem at Christmas?
SHERI	I know—shepherds!

> *She lunges forward and grabs Father's shoulder, creating a scene similar to the one with Garry. Father regains control of the car as Sheri speaks her next lines.*

	The shepherds came to Bethlehem! They heard the angels and they came looking for Jesus.
FATHER	Absolutely. Not a real *long* journey, but still a journey.

> *Lights fade on car as one or more members of the chorus reads from the NIV translation of Luke 2:8–16.*

READER	And there were shepherds living out in the fields nearby, keeping watch over their flocks at night. An angel of the Lord appeared to them, and the glory of the Lord shone around them, and they were terrified.
READER	But the angel said to them, "Do not be afraid. I bring you good news of great joy that will be for all the people. Today in the town of David a Savior has been born to you; he is Christ the Lord. This will be a sign to you: You will find a baby wrapped in strips of cloth and lying in a manger."

Destination Bethlehem

READER	Suddenly a great company of the heavenly host appeared with the angel, praising God and saying, "Glory to God in the highest, and on earth peace to men on whom his favor rests."
READER	When the angels had left them and gone into heaven, the shepherds said to one another, "Let's go to Bethlehem and see this thing that has happened, which the Lord has told us about." So they hurried off and found Mary and Joseph, and the baby, who was lying in the manger.
CHORUS	(*sings* Angels We Have Heard on High)

> *As chorus is singing, a number of male and female shepherds, perhaps as many as ten, enter from the back of the auditorium and make their way slowly down one or more of the aisles on their way to Bethlehem. They appear slightly confused as they whisper to one another and look left and right, searching for the child spoken of by the angels. Finally, near the end of the song, two of them notice Joseph and Mary and begin pointing toward them, motioning to the other shepherds as if to say: Here, this way! We've found the place! They then take positions around the manger, freezing in various positions of awe and amazement as lights come up again on car.*

FATHER	Okay—we've got Mary and Joseph and now the shepherds. Anyone figure out the third journey to Bethlehem?

> *Mother beckons for Garry to lean forward. As she whispers into his ear, she points a finger toward Terry, indicating that she wishes to help her answer part three of the riddle. Garry then whispers to Sheri, who whispers to an increasingly excited Terry. Terry then stands up and, while making her announcement with great enthusiasm, reaches around Father's head and puts a hand over each eye, creating yet another moment of panic for the beleaguered driver.*

TERRY	Magpie! (*they laugh*)
MOTHER	Ma-gi.
TERRY	Magi.
FATHER	(*in control again*) Magi is absolutely right! The wise men came to Bethlehem looking for the Christ child.

> *Lights fade on car as one or more members of the chorus read from the NIV translation of Matthew 2:1–5, 7–10.*

READER	After Jesus was born in Bethlehem . . . Magi from the east came to Jerusalem

	and asked, "Where is the one who has been born king of the Jews? We saw his star in the east and have come to worship him."
READER	When King Herod heard this he was disturbed, and all Jerusalem with him. When he had called together all the people's chief priests and teachers of the law, he asked them where the Christ was to be born. "In Bethlehem in Judea," they replied . . .
READER	Then Herod called the Magi secretly and found out from them the exact time the star had appeared. He sent them to Bethlehem and said, "Go and make a careful search for the child. As soon as you find him, report to me, so that I too may go and worship him."
READER	After they had heard the king, they went on their way, and the star they had seen in the east went ahead of them until it stopped over the place where the child was. When they saw the star, they were overjoyed.
CHORUS	(sings With a Star That Bright)
CHORUS	(sings We Three Kings of Orient Are)

This scene can be festive and joyful or simple and subdued. You may wish to eliminate all but the three wise men and even cut the first song altogether. Or, be bold and try it this way: As the chorus sings the first song, a caravan enters from the back of the church and journeys down an aisle toward the manger scene. At the rear are three or more wise men preceded by any number of servants, singers, and instrumentalists. They carry gifts, banners, streamers, trumpets, tambourines, lanterns, glow-in-the-dark objects of all kinds, and anything else you can think of to make it an exciting and memorable scene. You may even want to have a female angel leading the caravan, bearing a bright silver star high in the air, perhaps on a thin rod. If it is acceptable in your congregation, this angel could also be a dancer, leading the caravan in a creative, flowing expression of praise and exuberance. By the end of the first song, the procession will probably have arrived at the manger scene.

If you wish to extend the journey through the second song, they could continue their march by proceeding up and down another couple aisles, thus allowing in the process a close-up view of the caravan by the entire congregation. Whenever it comes, the end of the procession should leave at least the wise men in the vicinity of the manger. Arrange the other members of the caravan behind or to the sides, or sitting down in front, depending on the size of your stage. If you prefer not to extend the procession through the second song, it can be sung from these positions. You may even wish the wise men to sing solos. During the

Destination Bethlehem

song they also may present their gifts to Mary and Joseph. As the second song ends, the lights come up on the car and all in manger scene freeze.

FATHER — Not bad. Not bad at all. We got three of them right off the bat. But the fourth journey to Bethlehem—that's the tough one to figure out.

GARRY — Who else came at Christmas?

SHERI — I'm sure *I* don't know.

TERRY — I'm sure *I* don't know.

MOTHER — You've got *me* stumped, too. We've got Mary and Joseph coming from Nazareth, the shepherds coming from the fields outside the city, and the magi coming from the East. Who else? *(gasps)* Ohhhh! I know! Jesus came down from *heaven*! That's it—isn't it!

In her excitement over realizing the answer she has lunged toward Father and grabbed his right arm with both her hands and once again the poor guy has to struggle for a moment to keep the car on the road. He gains control again before answering.

FATHER — Yes, that's it. Jesus came down from heaven to be born a baby in Bethlehem.

Lights fade on car as one or two members of the chorus read from the NIV translation of John 1:1–2, 14; and Philippians 2:5–7.

READER —
In the beginning was the Word,
and the Word was with God,
and the Word was God.
He was with God in the beginning.

READER —
The Word became flesh and
lived for a while among us.

READER —
Your attitude should be the same
as that of Christ Jesus: Who,
being in very nature God,
did not consider equality with God
something to be grasped,
but made himself nothing,
taking on the very nature of a servant,
being made in human likeness.

CHORUS — *(sings* The Virgin Mary Had a Baby Boy*)*

As the chorus sings, an angel appears carrying the baby Jesus wrapped in the traditional swaddling clothes. She will eventually place him in the manger that Joseph has prepared, but the delivery may be as long and elaborate as desired, taking the entire length of the song if you wish. The angel may be accompanied by several other angels, and they may come down an aisle, down a staircase if one is available, or from somewhere on stage; if your church has a permanent raised pulpit, she might appear from there and then make her descent. If you are feeling adventurous and if liturgical dance is acceptable at your place of worship, the angel carrying the baby could perform a sort of "Bethlehem Ballet," spinning and striding gracefully across the stage or down the aisle in time with the music. After the baby is placed in the manger, the scene comes to life and the visitors whisper to one another, point, crane their necks to see, etc. The angel or angels can take positions behind the scene, or above if there is a choir loft. Following the next song, the lights will come up on the car as before.

CHORUS	(*sings* Ring the Bells)
FATHER	Well—pretty good job, you guys. You took care of that riddle like it was a piece of cake.
TERRY	(*her face next to his*) Cake?
MOTHER	(*up to something*) It's not over yet.
FATHER	Huh? Wha'd'you mean?
MOTHER	Well, you said there were four Christmas journeys. I can think of another one.
FATHER	(*perplexed*) A fifth journey?
MOTHER	Uh-huh. Who else journeys to Bethlehem at Christmas?
FATHER	Hmmm. Who else journeys to Bethlehem at Christmas? Boy, you got me on that one. Any ideas from back there?
GARRY	I don't know. I'm just wondering when *this* journey's gonna be over.
FATHER	(*lights up*) That's it! *We're* the ones who make the fifth journey!

He has let go of the steering wheel and is talking with his hands. He suddenly realizes what he's done and, with a look of horror, grabs hold of the wheel again and fights for a moment to regain control of the car.

FATHER	*We* have to journey to Bethlehem, too!
MOTHER	Yes. Jesus came down from heaven to bring us to God, but it's not enough for us to just *know* about that. Each one of us must make a personal journey to Jesus to receive the forgiveness and salvation that only he can give.

Lights fade on car as members of the chorus read the NIV translation of John 6:35, 37–40.

READER	Then Jesus declared, "I am the bread of life. He who comes to me will never go hungry, and he who believes in me will never be thirsty . . . All that the Father gives me will come to me, and whoever comes to me I will never drive away.
READER	For I have come down from heaven not to do my will but to do the will of him who sent me. And this is the will of him who sent me . . .

	that everyone who looks to the Son and believes in him shall have eternal life."
SINGER	*(sings* I Wonder As I Wander*)*
	(alternate solo: Joy in the Journey *by Michael Card)*
	The Singer enters hitchhiking on the car's right. He is carrying a suitcase and also a piece of cardboard on which is printed the words CITY OF GOD *or* HEAVENLY MANSION *or* FOOT OF THE CROSS *or* HOME, SWEET HOME. *If possible he should be lit by spotlight during the opening of the song while the rest of the stage is dark. The light widens to include the car as Father mimes pulling over to the side of the road. The children slide over to make room for the hitchhiker in the back seat, Terry sitting on Sheri's lap if necessary. The hitchhiker continues singing as Father begins driving again. Toward the end of the song, Father pulls over again and the Singer gets out of the car. He finishes the song at the side of the road; he is alone in the spotlight again as the song ends. After he exits, the set remains in darkness for a few moments. When the lights come up again the family has arrived at their destination.*
FATHER	We're here!
	After the children let out a cheer, Father mimes pressing the horn.
CHORUS	Beep beeeeep!
	They pile out of the car and head across the stage toward Grandma's house. Whether or not an actual grandmother steps out of the wing to greet them is up to you. If she's there, the children run into her arms; otherwise they run offstage. In either case, they are shouting "Grandma!" as they go. Mother and Father follow, but halfway across the stage they both stop and look at each other for a moment. Then Father runs back to the car, grabs the car seat, and returns to Mother's side. They smile and hurry to the same exit the children used.
PASTOR	*(shares message or closing)*
	At this point, your pastor might share a few words in closing. The topic could be the need for each of us to make a personal journey to Jesus, coming to him humbly as a child, asking for forgiveness and a new beginning.
CHORUS	*(sings* Celebrate the Season*)*
	As chorus and members of the manger scene sing, they begin to exit down the aisles.
FINALE	*(audience sings* O Come, All Ye Faithful*)*

Did I Miss Anything Important?

> This was true in Jesus' day too. The people prayed for deliverance, but most of them didn't have eyes to see the outrageous surprise God sent, for it shattered all their religious perceptions and expectations.
>
> Harold L. Myra
> *Living by God's Surprises*

Subject

Missing God's salvation.

Setting

Podium, chorus, and empty space.

Summary

1. Two narrators introduce the subject of failing to recognize God's deliverance.
2. Three of Noah's contemporaries discuss the weather, unaware that their neighbor's strange construction project is the means to God's deliverance.
3. Two soldiers in Saul's army take the day off because not much seems to be happening on the battlefield. Meanwhile, David is loading his slingshot.
4. A shepherd near Bethlehem keeps watch over the sheep while his cohorts hurry into town to look for the Christ child.
5. The wives of the wise men wonder why in the world their husbands went off to another country.
6. While the chorus sings, young actors form a nativity scene.

Characters

NARRATOR A, *female*
NARRATOR B, *male*
NEIGHBOR 1, *male or female*
NEIGHBOR 2, *male or female*
NEIGHBOR 3, *male or female*
SOLDIER 1, *male*
SOLDIER 2, *male*
SHEPHERD, *male*
MRS. MAGI, *female*
MRS. KING, *female*
MRS. WISE, *female*
READERS, *any number*
CHORUS

Nativity scene:

MARY
JOSEPH
SHEPHERDS
WISE MEN

Destination Bethlehem

There is no particular set required, just a podium at which the narrators can speak, a place from which the chorus can sing, and a spot in which the actors can act. For a prelude to the program using your youngest children, see the notes to the director at the end of the play.

NARRATOR A Good evening. My name is _____ and I'd like to welcome you to —

She is interrupted by a door slamming offstage or from the back of the auditorium. During the following moments, she will often look up from her script in the direction of the disturbance.

And I'd like to welcome you to this year's—

She is distracted again: The person who slammed the door is running, or at least hurrying, up the aisle or across the stage, making plenty of noise as he comes. Perhaps the noise is in the form of running into an empty chair, or in bumping into a prewarned member of the audience with a loud "Excuse me!" being heard by everyone.

To this year's Christmas program, presented by _____. The title of this year's program is—

The disruptive person, who is actually Narrator B, is approaching the podium, puffing loudly.

As I was saying, the title of this year's program is—

Narrator B cuts her off by speaking into the microphone.

NARRATOR B Did I Miss Anything Important?

NARRATOR A *(quietly)* Only my introduction. But you *could* have been on time. We *are* in front of hundreds of people, you know. Now if you'll excuse me, I have to get back to the script. *(reads again)* The title of this year's program is—

NARRATOR B Did I Miss Anything Important?

NARRATOR A *(becoming annoyed)* I just told you. A couple of sentences—nothing major. Now please be quiet and let me finish. The title of this—

NARRATOR B *(interrupting)* You don't understand. That *is* the title.

NARRATOR A *What's* the title?

NARRATOR B What I just said. It's my line. You were supposed to read *those* lines *(points to page)* and then I was supposed to read the title and *these* lines.

Narrator A reads rapidly to herself, just loud enough for the audience to overhear.

NARRATOR A Good evening, my name is hm-hmm, and I'd like to welcome you to this year's Christmas program, presented by hm-hmmm, the title of this year's program is—

TOGETHER Did I Miss Anything Important?

NARRATOR A Oh—you're right. I guess I should have read the script ahead of time. *(considers)* Strange title if you ask me.

NARRATOR B It's a program about some people who might have lived back in Bible times, who chose to stay behind when significant things were happening in the world around them.

NARRATOR A	Sounds interesting. Can you give me an example?
NARRATOR B	Sure. Here's one now.

One or more readers from the chorus read from the NIV translation of Genesis 6:5–19 and 7:5.

READER(S)
The LORD saw how great man's wickedness
on the earth had become, and that every
inclination of the thoughts of his heart
was only evil all the time. The LORD was
grieved that he had made man on the earth,
and his heart was filled with pain . . .
But Noah found favor in the eyes of the LORD . . .
Noah was a righteous man, blameless
among the people of his time, and he walked
with God . . . So God said to Noah, "I am going
to put an end to all people, for the earth
is filled with violence because of them . . .
So make yourself an ark of cypress wood;
make rooms in it and coat it with pitch
inside and out . . . Put a door in the side
of the ark and make lower, middle, and upper
decks. I am going to bring floodwaters
on the earth to destroy all life under
the heavens, every creature that has
the breath of life in it . . . But I will establish
my covenant with you, and you will enter
the ark—you and your sons and your wife
and your sons' wives with you. You are
to bring into the ark two of all living
creatures, male and female, to keep them
alive with you. . . ." And Noah did all
that the LORD commanded him.

Lights come up on three of Noah's neighbors, dressed in Bible costumes but carrying modern umbrellas. If you don't feel comfortable with this combination, they can just hold out their headpieces above themselves as though trying to stay dry. The sound of thunder or rain as the scene begins would be appropriate, but be careful that it doesn't continue through the scene and drown out the dialogue.

NEIGHBOR 1	*(squinting upward)* Strange weather.
NEIGHBOR 2	Yeah. I wonder what you call it.
NEIGHBOR 3	*(shrugs)* Anything you want to. It's never *happened* before.
NEIGHBOR 2	Then let's call it a "pour-down."
NEIGHBOR 1	A pour-down? *(considers)* Why not a "downpour"?
NEIGHBOR 2	What's the difference?

NEIGHBOR 1	I have no idea.
NEIGHBOR 2	Then why not just call it a pour-down?
NEIGHBOR 1	*(sighs)* Fine.
NEIGHBOR 3	*(gazing skyward)* Looks like *rain* to me.
NEIGHBOR 2	Rain?
NEIGHBOR 1	Rain?
NEIGHBOR 3	Rain. Just a word I made up. Kind of wet, drippy stuff falling from the sky like, like—
NEIGHBOR 2	Like hens and horses?
NEIGHBOR 3	No, more like—
NEIGHBOR 1	Like pigs and parakeets?
NEIGHBOR 3	No, more like . . . like cats and dogs.
NEIGHBOR 2	*Cats and dogs?*
NEIGHBOR 1	Get real.
NEIGHBOR 2	Hey, speaking of animals, did you guys hear about all the animals Noah was loading up on that floating barn of his?
NEIGHBOR 1	Didn't have to *hear* about it. I can *smell* it all the way across the valley!
NEIGHBOR 2	*(shaking his head)* Poor fella's gone off the deep end.
NEIGHBOR 1	Guy oughta be arrested, if you ask me.
NEIGHBOR 2	He's all wet, that's for sure.
NEIGHBOR 3	And we're not?

They give him a look, then begin exiting following the next line.

NEIGHBOR 1	Let's go find a nice dry spot, okay?
NEIGHBOR 2	Yeah. Otherwise somebody will be sayin' we don't have enough sense to come in out of the pour-down.
NEIGHBOR 1	So how long do you think this'll last?
NEIGHBOR 3	Long time, I'm afraid.
NEIGHBOR 2	Nah. Couple hours at the most.
NEIGHBOR 1	Good. Afterwards let's go over and give ol' Noah a hard time—whad'ya say?
NEIGHBOR 2	Sounds like fun.

They exit and lights come up again on the two narrators. Narrator B is still looking off toward where the actors exited.

NARRATOR A	*(reading)* So, did they miss anything important?
NARRATOR B	*(after a bit)* Huh?

NARRATOR A	The title of the program, remember?
NARRATOR B	Oh—
NARRATOR A	What did they miss?
NARRATOR B	They missed the boat, that's for sure.
NARRATOR A	Exactly. They missed the deliverance of God.
NARRATOR B	The what?
CHORUS	(loudly) THE DELIVERANCE OF GOD!

Narrator B nearly falls over—or perhaps he actually does. Because of his late entrance he hadn't noticed the presence of the chorus. He gathers his wits about him or brushes himself off, then listens to the song.

CHORUS	(sings Noah [Arky, Arky])
NARRATOR B	Oh, the deliverance of God.
NARRATOR A	Yes.
NARRATOR B	Any other examples of people who missed the boat?
NARRATOR A	Well, not a boat this time, but something important.
NARRATOR B	Let me have it.
NARRATOR A	Okay, here it comes.

One or more readers from the chorus read from the NIV translation of 1 Samuel 17:2–16.

READER(S)	Saul and the Israelites assembled . . . and drew up their battle line to meet the Philistines . . . A champion named Goliath . . . came out of the Philistine camp. He was over nine feet tall. He had a bronze helmet on his head and wore a coat of . . . bronze weighing [about 125 pounds] . . . Goliath stood and shouted to the ranks of Israel, "Why do you come out and line up for battle? . . . Choose a man and have him come down to me. If he is able to fight and kill me, we will become your subjects; but if I overcome him and kill him, you will become our subjects . . ." On hearing the Philistine's words, Saul and all the Israelites were dismayed and terrified . . . For forty days the Philistine came forward every morning and evening and took his stand.

Lights come up on two soldiers. The first is dozing; the second has just entered and is cautiously glancing behind him as he crosses the stage.

SOLDIER 1	(waking) So, you didn't go out to fight today, either?

SOLDIER 2	Nah. I'm getting tired of fighting the Philistines. I called in sick.
SOLDIER 1	Yeah, me too.
SOLDIER 2	Besides, it'll just be another day of listening to that big guy—what's his name again?
SOLDIER 1	Goliath.
SOLDIER 2	It'll just be another day of listening to Goliath boasting and taunting. It gets old real fast.
SOLDIER 1	*(yawns)* Tell me about it.
SOLDIER 2	By the way, I passed that shepherd kid on the way here—Jesse's boy? He said to say hi.
SOLDIER 1	Little David? What's *he* doing out here?
SOLDIER 2	He's taking a sack lunch out to his brothers.
SOLDIER 1	I hope he's careful. The battlefield's no place for a harp player.
SOLDIER 2	Hey, listen to this. I told him Goliath had issued a challenge to fight any one man, winner take all, and David says he'd like to have a crack at the guy with his slingshot!

They roar with laughter.

SOLDIER 1	That's a good one! Almost be worth it to go out there and watch.
SOLDIER 2	Are you kidding? I just pressed these pants! I'm not gonna go out there and get 'em all wrinkled!
SOLDIER 1	Well, then, have a seat. It's gonna be a long afternoon without much happening.
SOLDIER 2	Thanks, don't mind if I do. *(sits)* Hey—got any chips?

Lights fade on soldiers and come up again on narrators.

NARRATOR A	So—did they miss anything important?
NARRATOR B	Yes! *(proud that he knows the answer)*
NARRATOR A	What did they miss?
NARRATOR B	The de—
CHORUS	*(drowning him out)* THE DELIVERANCE OF GOD!

He's knocked for a loop again by the outburst and again gathers himself together as the chorus sings.

CHORUS	*(sings* Only a Boy Named David*)*
NARRATOR B	Well, this is becoming very interesting. Any more examples of people missing out on something important?
NARRATOR A	Lots of them, but since it's Christmas, maybe we should move ahead to something more in keeping with the season. Let's see—

As though throwing away her script, she tosses a stack of blank pages on the floor. Narrator B is slightly aghast.

NARRATOR A Don't look so shocked. The Bible is *full* of people who missed the chance to enjoy the blessings that God wanted to give them.

NARRATOR B Like who?

NARRATOR A *(whispers)* We don't have time.

NARRATOR B *(whispers)* Just name a couple.

She rolls her eyes, then picks up papers from the floor and glances through them.

NARRATOR A *(still low)* Samson.

NARRATOR B *(still low)* Uh-huh.

NARRATOR A Saul.

NARRATOR B Oh yeah.

NARRATOR A Solomon.

NARRATOR B *(louder)* King Solomon?

NARRATOR A *(louder)* Yes, even King Solomon missed the boat. Toward the end of his life, that is.

NARRATOR B Hmmm.

NARRATOR A But we really must move on. *(sets pages aside)*

NARRATOR B Fine. Who's next?

NARRATOR A Well, like I said, since it's Christmas . . .

One or more readers from the chorus read from the NIV translation of Luke 2:8–15.

READER(S) And there were shepherds living out
in the fields nearby, keeping watch over
their flocks at night. An angel of the Lord
appeared to them, and the glory of the Lord
shone around them, and they were terrified.
But the angel said to them, "Do not be afraid.
I bring you good news of great joy that will be
for all the people. Today in the town of David
a Savior has been born to you; he is Christ the Lord.
This will be a sign to you: You will find a baby
wrapped in strips of cloth and lying in a manger."
Suddenly a great company of the heavenly host
appeared with the angel, praising God . . .
When the angels had left them and gone into heaven,
the shepherds said to one another, "Let's go
to Bethlehem and see this thing that has happened,
which the Lord has told us about."

Destination Bethlehem

Lights come up on a lonely shepherd, sitting with staff in hand on a rock. He wears traditional shepherd clothing, including a headpiece.

SHEPHERD Achooo! Aaachoo!

He looks around for a tissue, realizes they haven't been invented yet, so wipes his nose on his headpiece. After a moment he notices audience.

Oh—hi there. I'm just *(sniffs)* trying to get over this head cold. Actually, I'm just coming down with it. Well, actually, I think it's more of an allergy. I think—*(looks around)* I think I'm allergic to sheep. Not a good situation to be in if you're a shepherd, is it. Oh well, it could be worse. I could be allergic to my wife, for instance. *(ponders)* Actually, I think I *am* allergic to her. She breaks out in hives whenever I'm around. *(scratches his head)* You're probably wondering where the other shepherds are tonight. Well, they all went suddenly into town. *(looks off)* Bethlehem. I was sleeping over there when I was awakened by a commotion. By the time my head had cleared enough for me to figure out what was going on, the other shepherds were all in a frenzy over which one of them would stay here with the sheep while the rest of them ran into town for something. *(shrugs)* I'm not sure what. Anyway, right about then I sneezed and they thought I had volunteered to stay, so here I am.

He sneezes again, then looks off toward the town of Bethlehem.

Oh well, what's another trip to Bethlehem? Can't be anything *too* important, can it?

Lights fade out on shepherd and up again on narrators.

NARRATOR A So—what did he miss?

Narrator B grimaces, puts his hands over his ears, and ducks, preparing himself for another outburst from the chorus. But they make not a sound. After a moment or two, he uncovers his ears, looks around and stands up, relaxed. The chorus chooses just that moment to shout louder than ever.

CHORUS THE DELIVERANCE OF GOD!

Narrator B does his thing, then recovers again as chorus sings.

CHORUS (*sings* The First Noel)

NARRATOR B So, what's next?

NARRATOR A Oh, some women who may not have really existed but might have.

NARRATOR B Hmmm. I wonder who they could be.

One or more readers from the chorus read from the NIV translation of Matthew 2:1–10.

READERS After Jesus was born in Bethlehem . . .
Magi from the east came to Jerusalem
and asked, "Where is the one who has
been born king of the Jews? We saw
his star in the east and have come
to worship him." When King Herod
heard this he was disturbed, and all
Jerusalem with him. When he had called

together all the people's chief priests
and teachers of the law, he asked them
where the Christ was to be born.
In Bethlehem in Judea, they replied . . .
Then Herod called the Magi secretly
and found out from them the exact time
the star had appeared. He sent them
to Bethlehem and said, "Go and make
a careful search for the child.
As soon as you find him, report to me,
so that I too may go and worship him."
After they had heard the king, they went
on their way, and the star they had seen
in the east went ahead of them until it stopped
over the place where the child was.
When they saw the star, they were overjoyed.

Lights come up on three women dressed in elaborate clothing and looking out across the desert toward Judea.

MRS. KING	What do you think, ladies? Are they ever coming back? It's been three months now.
MRS. MAGI	*(agreeing)* Two months and twenty-seven days.
MRS. KING	*(misunderstanding)* Well, it *seems* like three months!
MRS. WISE	I wonder if they've found what they were looking for.
MRS. KING	*(not hearing her)* Think of it! A little star twinkles in the sky and they go traipsing off to some ridiculous foreign country that probably hasn't even invented perfume yet. *(looks at sky)* Some itsy-bitsy speck of light out there who-knows-how-high-up, probably twenty miles or more, so small it couldn't shine its way through a slight overcast, and the three of them pack up and leave like it was the most important journey of their lives.
MRS. WISE	Perhaps it *is* important.
MRS. KING	Next year's *fashions* are important. Stars come and go.
MRS. MAGI	I don't know about that. Why just the other day I heard my great-grandfather say something about the stars being exactly the same today as they were when he was a boy.
MRS. KING	The old coot can't see past his nose. What does *he* know?
MRS. WISE	*(looking skyward)* Our husbands seem to think the heavens have some significance.
MRS. KING	I have more important things beneath my living room *rug* than my husband could ever find up in the sky! Don't give me that stuff about significance! I think he was just trying to get out of town.
MRS. WISE	*(under her breath)* I wonder why.
MRS. KING	*(overhearing)* What's that?

MRS. WISE	Nothing. I was just wondering why they'd want to leave their loving families behind, that's all.
MRS. KING	Oh, you know men. They always think the grass is greener on the other side of the oasis.
MRS. MAGI	Maybe we should have gone with them.
	She steps away from them and looks off longingly in the direction of Judea.
MRS. KING	What? And miss the big end-of-the-year sale down at the Five-and-Drachma?
MRS. MAGI	*(sarcastic but not unkind)* We wouldn't want to miss something that important, would we?
MRS. WISE	No. We wouldn't want to miss something important.
	She has joined Mrs. Magi in gazing toward Judea. Lights fade on the three women and come up on chorus.
CHORUS	*(sings* O Little Town of Bethlehem*)*
	As chorus sings, Mary, Joseph, and a group of shepherds enter and form a nativity scene.
CHORUS	*(sings* With a Star That Bright*)*
	As the chorus sings, wise men enter and take traditional nativity-scene positions. If you wish to add more songs to the program, this would be the appropriate spot. At some point during the music, possibly immediately following the wise men's entrance, the two narrators join the nativity scene.
CHORUS	*(sings* Rise, Come and See the King*)*
PASTOR	*(Shares a few thoughts or perhaps an entire sermon on how some people miss the deliverance of God in the person of his Son who came at Christmas to bring salvation to all who would open their hearts to his love and forgiveness.)*
	If the pastor's message is brief, you may want to save the preceding choral offering until after he is through; otherwise the program can end on a Christmas carol with audience participation.
FINALE	*(all sing* Joy to the World*)*

Notes to the Director

If you are including younger children who are likely to become restless sitting through the drama portions of this program, you may want to bring them out ahead of time to sing some or all of the following songs:

O Come, Little Children
Bring a Torch, Jeanette, Isabella
Go Tell It on the Mountain
Assurance March
Silent Night
Jesus Loves Even Me
Into My Heart

If you need to shorten this program, and if you feel that most of the people in your audience are familiar with the stories of Noah's ark, David and Goliath, and the shepherds and wise men, the program will work fine without the Scripture readings.

You may wish to substitute the phrase "salvation of God" for "deliverance of God."

R.S.V.P.

> Abiding in Christ . . . will mean arranging life, arranging prayer, arranging silence in such a way that there is never a day when we give ourselves a chance to forget Him.
>
> William Barclay
> *The Gospel of John*

Subject

Being responsive to God.

Setting

A grandmother in a rocking chair. Life-size Christmas card replicas.

Summary

1. Young children carry oversized envelopes that spell out the word *Christmas*.

2. The postman delivers Grandma's mail, including plenty of Christmas cards.

3. Grandma invites the audience in for a chat and shows them some of her Christmas cards. As she does so, three of the cards are seen in life-size replica: Mary and Joseph on their way to Bethlehem, the shepherds listening to the angel, the wise men following the star.

4. Grandma shares another card that speaks of our need to be responsive to God.

5. The characters in the Christmas cards come to life for a few moments to demonstrate what it might have been like if the people in the Christmas story had not been interested in God's plan for their lives.

6. Grandma explains that those people really *did* respond to God. As the chorus sings the Christmas story, the characters from the first three cards combine to create a fourth card: a nativity scene.

7. A soloist sings a song about responding to the call of Christ.

Characters

GRANDMA, *main character, many lines; could be played by an adult*
POSTMAN, *could be played by an adult; good whistler*
JOSEPH, *nonspeaking part*
MARY, *brief speaking part*
ANGEL, *nonspeaking part*
SHEPHERDS, *two or more; one speaking part*
MAGI 1, *brief speaking part*
MAGI 2, *brief speaking part*
MAGI 3, *nonspeaking part*
CHORUS
SOLOIST

Destination Bethlehem

When lights come up, Grandma sits dozing in a rocking chair. Along with a basketful of Christmas cards and perhaps a small table with a lamp on it, this is all that is essential for the set. However, you may wish to build a kitchen or living room around her or suggest those rooms with a few more pieces of furniture and suitable props. Christmas cards taped to the wall or placed on furniture would of course help set the scene for this particular program. Somewhere, off to the side or behind the set, is an area for a chorus of children, either all present at the same time or brought in group by group for different songs.

For now, though, all that really matters is this: Nine of your youngest children have entered and are standing in a line across the front of the stage. Each of them carries a very large white envelope. These are Christmas cards ready for mailing and they bear Grandma's address (or perhaps just her name) and a large simulated postage stamp. On the reverse side of each envelope, not as yet visible to the audience, is a large individual letter of the alphabet. When the envelopes are turned around at the appropriate moments in the song, the audience will be able to read the word Christmas.

CHORUS (*sings* Love Letters of Christmas)

Following the song, the children exit, possibly dropping the cards in an oversized mailbox along the way. From the back of the auditorium we hear someone whistling I'm Dreaming of a White Christmas. *It is the postman delivering the mail. As he makes his way up the middle aisle he stops every few rows to lighten his pouch of a handful of envelopes: either dropping them into a series of homemade mailboxes that have been attached to some of the pews or handing them to audience members sitting at the end of the row. As he nears the front, Grandma hears him whistling and wakes up. She goes to the window and looks out, smiles, then goes to the door to be there when he arrives with the mail.*

POSTMAN Morning, Mrs. Everett.

GRANDMA Hello, Mr. Adams. Looks like we're in for some snow.

POSTMAN In for a whole lot of it, I hear.

GRANDMA Just so it doesn't stop the mail.

POSTMAN Never! You know the old saying.

GRANDMA Yes. I think it would take the second coming to stop you from getting me my mail. And always right on time.

POSTMAN Well, we can't have you missing out on your Christmas cards, now, can we? Got quite a few of them for you again today. (*hands them to her*)

GRANDMA Mercy!

POSTMAN You're the most popular person on my route, Mrs. Everett.

GRANDMA It's called having lots of grandchildren. Ohhh, when I get these cards, it's like each and every one of those little darlings is right here with me.

Immediately the lights come up on children's chorus, and the song begins. Postman continues on his way with a wave. Grandma waves after him, closes the door and takes the envelopes to her chair where she begins opening them and reading the cards.

CHORUS	(*sings* Over the River and through the Woods)
CHORUS	(*sings* We Wish You a Merry Christmas)

This would be a convenient spot for the chorus to exit if various groups are being brought in. Following the song, Grandma looks up and notices the audience, then addresses them.

GRANDMA Oh—hello. I didn't see you come in. Can I get you something to drink? A cup of hot tea? Some eggnog? I've got plenty. No? Well, why don't you just sit down there and make yourself comfortable and we'll have a nice chat. (*notices cards*) Say, now, isn't this just about the best time of the year? It's the only time other than my birthday when the bills and junk mail are outnumbered by the good stuff—you know, cards and letters. (*takes basket*) I really do love Christmas cards. Look at this one—kind of nice, don'tcha think? It's from my grandson Jacob. Of course, he's too young to have sent it himself. His mother, my daughter Emily, did all the work—but that's his scribbling—I'd recognize it anywhere. (*chuckles*) Now here's one that's really pretty. From my son Jeremy and his wife Darlene. It's a painting of Joseph and Mary on their way to Bethlehem.

Lights come up on a life-size Christmas card: Joseph and Mary standing side by side, as though walking along a road. If you do not have complex lighting capabilities, just have Joseph and Mary enter and freeze when they come to the right spot. If possible, there should be some kind of background to indicate a Christmas card, perhaps a wooden rectangular frame for its outer edge, or a painted rectangular backdrop or screen.

GRANDMA (*holding up card*) And here's a nice one from my Grandson Cody: the shepherds listening in amazement to the angel.

Lights come up on another life-size Christmas card: two or more shepherds listening to an angel. None of them move.

And here's one I really like: Kelly, my granddaughter from Topeka—Kansas—always sends me a card with the wise men following the star.

Lights come up on a third life-size Christmas card: the magi looking heavenward. They do not move.

GRANDMA (*searching*) But the one I *really* want to tell you about—I actually got it several years ago, but I always bring it out again every Christmas—here it is. It's from my granddaughter Erika—she's in college now—Florida State. It doesn't have a pretty picture or anything—but the words are so special. Here, let me read it to you: "Have you ever wondered why God announced the greatest birth in human history to a handful of shepherds on a hillside and a few wise men from the East? Perhaps it was because they were quiet enough to listen, eager enough to know, and available enough to follow." (*stops reading*) I've thought about those words quite often since I got this card. Especially when I hear about people who don't think Christmas is very important. Or maybe they know Christmas is somehow important—that it has something to do with God—but then the rest of the year they don't give him another thought. Or sometimes I'll meet people who *know* that God is important all year round, but they're just too busy to ever stop and find out what he might be trying to say to them. And then I think—what if the people in the Christmas story had acted that way? What if the wise men, for instance, weren't really interested in where God wanted to lead them?

Lights come up on the third Christmas card. The wise man on the right turns and speaks to the wise man in the middle, who doesn't seem to be too interested.

MAGI 1   There's a new star in the sky tonight. It seems to be beckoning for us to follow it.

MAGI 2   Oh, that's cool. (*turns to third wise man*) Now, as I was saying, there I was in the middle of the desert with a dehydrated camel. Can you believe it? I'm telling you, my luck just hasn't been going too well lately.

The lights on the third card fade and its members freeze again.

GRANDMA   Or what if, when the angel came and announced the birth of the Christ child, the shepherds were just too busy to be bothered?

Lights come up on the second Christmas card where one of the shepherds is talking to the astonished angel.

SHEPHERD   That's all well and good in theory, but we've got a major problem on our hands right now. Seems one of the lambs has an identity crisis. Can you maybe come back next week?

The lights on the second Christmas card fade and its members freeze again.

GRANDMA   Or take Mary, the mother of Jesus. When God told her she had been chosen to bear his only Son, what if she was just not in the mood?

Lights come up on first Christmas card. Mary comes briefly to life, but Joseph may either remain frozen or look at her aghast.

MARY   (*upward*) I'm really not feeling very motherly at the moment. Could you try someone else?

The lights on the first Christmas card fade and its members freeze again.

GRANDMA   Well, of course it didn't happen that way, but I think you get the picture. Mary, as you know, said yes to the invitation to motherhood. She and Joseph traveled to Bethlehem to take part in the census, and while they were there, the time came for the baby's birth.

CHORUS   (*sings* Silent Night)

As the chorus sings, Mary and Joseph leave the first Christmas card and make their way to an area of the stage designated as the manger. They take traditional positions and then freeze, creating the beginnings of a fourth Christmas card.

CHORUS   (*sings* Away in a Manger *if another song is needed*)

GRANDMA   And the shepherds were not too busy to respond to the good news from God. They hurried into the city in search of the Savior.

CHORUS   (*sings* While Shepherds Watched Their Flocks)

	As the chorus sings, the shepherds leave the second Christmas card and journey to the manger where they take traditional positions and then freeze. The angel does the same but perhaps by a different route.
CHORUS	(*sings* The First Noel *if another song is needed*)
GRANDMA	And we all know that the wise men were very interested in the unusual star they saw. *So* interested that they went to a great deal of trouble to journey all the way to Bethlehem in search of the child who had been announced by the universe.
CHORUS	(*sings* With a Star That Bright)
	As the chorus sings, the wise men from the third Christmas card journey as far as your stage will allow—possibly up and down an aisle or two—before arriving at the manger scene. Once there they, too, take traditional positions and freeze, completing the fourth Christmas card.
SOLOIST	(*sings* Do You Hear What I Hear?)
GRANDMA	Oh, what a marvelous story! Isn't it wonderful what God will do when people are: quiet enough to listen, eager enough to know, and available enough to follow?
	She sets her special card on the table, then rises and exits.
PASTOR	(*shares message on responding to God*)
SOLOIST	(*sings* The Word *by Michael Card*)
FINALE	(*audience joins in on* Joy to the World)

Something Sacred This Way Comes

> There is a knowledge in the look of things,
> The old hills hunch before the north wind blows.
>
> Howard Nemerov
> *A Spell before Winter*

Subject

Advent. Waiting for Christ.

Setting

Any empty space will do.

Summary

1. An inquisitive girl questions a prophet who is waiting for his predictions concerning the Messiah to come true.

2. She next questions a shepherd boy who has heard something in the darkness and is waiting for it to show itself.

3. Finally, she questions a gentleman in elaborate clothing. He tells her he has seen something unusual in the sky and is waiting for the clouds to clear so he can study it further.

4. The girl, Inquisitoria, recalls for us the Virgin Mary who waited for the birth of her son Jesus.

5. As the chorus sings *Do You Hear What I Hear?* those on stage act out the words: the prophet becomes the night wind whispering to the shepherd boy's little lamb; the lamb gets the attention of her master, who in turn points out for the mighty king the child who has been born in the night.

6. Inquisitoria holds a child and all gather around her to form a nativity scene as the song ends.

Characters

INQUISITORIA, *female (could be male)*
NIGHT WIND, *male (could be female)*
SHEPHERD BOY, *male*
LITTLE LAMB, *male or female*
MIGHTY KING, *male*
CHORUS

First, nothing.

Then, slowly, an aging man in gray flowing robes enters and crosses to the left side of the stage (stage right), where he stops and looks off into the future, which in this case is a spot about fifteen feet above the floor on the back wall of the auditorium. His eyes never move from this spot. His name: Night Wind.

Enter, after a few seconds, a girl: Inquisitoria. She approaches the old man cautiously, uncertainly. She stops next to him, looks in the direction he is looking, looks back at him. Finally she speaks.

INQUISITORIA	Wha—what are you doing?
NIGHT WIND	Waiting.
INQUISITORIA	Waiting?
NIGHT WIND	Waiting.
INQUISITORIA	*(beat)* Waiting for what?
NIGHT WIND	I am a prophet. I wait for my predictions to come true.
INQUISITORIA	Well—what did you predict?
NIGHT WIND	Love.
INQUISITORIA	Love?
NIGHT WIND	Love. And joy, and peace, and hope, and forgiveness, and wisdom, and justice, and victory—and life.
INQUISITORIA	*(amazed)* All those things?
NIGHT WIND	*(considers)* Just one thing, actually. Just one.

He continues staring into the future. She looks with him in the same direction. They freeze as lights fade on them and come up on chorus.

CHORUS	*(sings* O Come, O Come, Emmanuel*)*

Lights fade on chorus and come up on stage. Enter the Shepherd Boy, warily searching the darkness around him, listening intently. At his side is Little Lamb—actually a child in partial or full costume. They come to a stop at least several yards to the left of Inquisitoria, who has noted with great interest their arrival. She approaches.

INQUISITORIA	*(loud)* Hello.
SHEPHERD BOY	*(urgently)* Shhh!
INQUISITORIA	*(whispering)* What is it? What's the matter?
SHEPHERD BOY	*(low)* The sheep sense that something is out there. *(indicates the darkness)*
INQUISITORIA	Something?
SHEPHERD BOY	Something.
INQUISITORIA	Like *what?*

Destination Bethlehem

SHEPHERD BOY	*(anxious)* I don't *know*.
INQUISITORIA	Aren't you going to go look for it?
SHEPHERD BOY	No. If I go out there, whatever it is might circle back here to the place where I am not, and my sheep would be in danger.
INQUISITORIA	So what will you do?
SHEPHERD BOY	Wait.
INQUISITORIA	Wait?
SHEPHERD BOY	Wait. *(determined)* I will wait until it shows itself, whatever it is.
INQUISITORIA	What do you *think* it is—an animal?
SHEPHERD BOY	*(not unfriendly)* Well of course. What else would it be? A choir of angels? Shhhh.
	He too freezes—staring into the darkness, listening—and is joined in this stance by Little Lamb and Inquisitoria. Lights fade on them and come up on chorus.
CHORUS	*(sings* While Shepherds Watched Their Flocks*)*
	Lights come up on stage. All but Inquisitoria remain frozen as the Mighty King enters and begins pacing back and forth. With each turn he pauses briefly and looks toward the sky. Inquisitoria has noticed him and begins following close behind him. Suddenly he stops to squint at the sky and she runs right into him.
MIGHTY KING	Wha—?
INQUISITORIA	*(bowing)* Your Excellency—I beg your pardon!
MIGHTY KING	*(kindly)* Nonsense. No harm intended, no pardon needed.
INQUISITORIA	*(rising)* Thank you, sir.
MIGHTY KING	I would, however, appreciate an explanation.
INQUISITORIA	Explanation?
MIGHTY KING	Explanation. I don't mind being bumped into, but I like to know why—and by whom.
INQUISITORIA	By whom is easy: It was me.
MIGHTY KING	*(amused)* Ah. Nice to meet me.
INQUISITORIA	*(curtsies)* Thank you. Now *why* I bumped into you is more difficult to explain. Lately I seem to be running into people who are waiting.
MIGHTY KING	Waiting?
INQUISITORIA	Waiting, yes. For what I'm not sure, but I think it is soon. And then I saw you pacing back and forth and looking toward the sky and I said to myself, here is a man who is waiting as well. *(beat)* Was I right?
MIGHTY KING	*(thoughtfully)* Yes. You are right. My partners and I are waiting for the clouds to clear. *(looks up)* They are asleep—it is my turn to observe. We thought earlier this evening that we noticed something different in the twilight sky. But just as we brought out

	our charts to compare what we saw tonight with what we've seen in the past, the clouds moved in. *(sighs)* So now we wait for clear skies.
INQUISITORIA	How long do you think that will take?
MIGHTY KING	Perhaps a few hours, maybe a few days. It is difficult to tell with clouds—they move with the wind, and the wind, as you are well aware, blows wherever it will. *(looks toward sky)* We are at the mercy of the wind....

He freezes, staring into the sky, as does Inquisitoria. Lights fade on them and come up on chorus.

CHORUS	*(sings* As with Gladness Men of Old*)*
	(alternate song: We Three Kings of Orient Are*)*

Following the song, all except Inquisitoria remain frozen as lights come up on them again. Prior to or during her next lines Inquisitoria walks to a spot several yards to the Mighty King's left. Now all on stage are equally spaced across the front: Night Wind stage right, then Shepherd Boy with Little Lamb, then Mighty King, then Inquisitoria. Her words are addressed to the audience.

INQUISITORIA	To a young woman from Nazareth
	there appeared one day an angel
	who announced to her
	that the God who was her Father
	would also be her son—and so,
	she waited for the miracle.

She too freezes, gazing reverently toward heaven. Lights do not fade during music.

CHORUS	*(sings* Do You Hear What I Hear?*)*

The following blend of mime and music can be very simple or very elaborate, depending on the talent available and the time you wish to invest. As the chorus sings, the words of the song are acted out by the five actors on stage. First, the Night Wind approaches Little Lamb, perhaps spinning around or dancing across the stage as he or she does so. Night Wind then points toward "a star shining in the night" and Little Lamb raises its eyes in awe and wonder. The Mighty King also turns and looks skyward at the "warm and heavenly light." Next, Little Lamb tugs on the sleeve of Shepherd Boy, who crouches down next to his furry friend. The lamb cups a hand behind her ear to indicate a song "ringing through the sky" and the eyes of her master tell us he too can hear the angels sing. Shepherd Boy then walks to Mighty King, bows, and points toward Inquisitoria, who has cradled an imaginary baby in her arms. Mighty King gazes in amazement at the child who "shivers in the cold." Inquisitoria carries her baby center stage where all gather around: Night Wind takes up a position like Joseph in nativity scenes, Shepherd Boy kneels on one knee to her right, Little Lamb lies down in front, Mighty King stands to Inquisitoria's left. Mighty King faces the audience and spreads his arms majestically, announcing to "people everywhere" the child who "will bring us goodness and light." All on stage freeze as song ends and lights fade out.

Nocturne

I could not sleep for thinking of the sky.
>John Masefield
>*(poem of same title)*

Subject

Why Christ came.

Setting

A dimly lit stage, divided chorus.

Summary

1. Nine stargazers venture into the night where they recite Bible verses about the splendor of the heavens.
2. The chorus hums *Silent Night*.
3. Two stargazers recite *O Little Town of Bethlehem*, then become Mary and Joseph in a manger scene.
4. Four more stargazers recite *In the Bleak Midwinter*, then become shepherds keeping watch over their flocks as a soloist sings *O Holy Night*.
5. The three remaining stargazers alternate with the divided chorus in reciting *We Three Kings of Orient Are*, then suddenly become three men being crucified; the stargazers in the manger scene simultaneously have become the crowd on Calvary.
6. Pastor speaks about the real purpose of Christ's coming.
7. Depending on solo chosen, the nine stargazers witness either the resurrection or second coming of Christ.

Characters

STARGAZERS, *nine of them. Of the first two, one must be male and the other female; the fifth should be male; the remainder may be male or female regardless of the role they play in the manger scene.*

CHORUS, *divided into Group A and Group B*

VOICE, *preferably male; amplified*

SOLOISTS, *four or less. One or more of the solos may be sung by the chorus if you wish. The solos may be performed by four different singers, or all by the same person, depending on availability and the style of the production.*

It is, most importantly, night.

Artificial stars twinkling overhead or in the background would help create the appropriate effect, but we can pretend if need be. On the left and on the right are set up platforms for the divided chorus. Center stage is the city of Bethlehem: perhaps an empty space that can be filled by the imagination, perhaps a painted backdrop, or perhaps a city in miniature, lights in the windows, lanterns at the doors.

It is into this night that the audience ventures, accompanied by the sounds of crickets and frogs.

And it is under this night that the stargazers gather, silently watching the sky as they come. Their clothing is uniform: simple, modern, and black. Their number is nine. Lining up along the upstage edge of the city, they form a half-moon arc open to the audience. (If the area designated Bethlehem were the face of a clock with the number six nearest the seats, the stargazers would be standing on the numbers eight through four; the first stargazer would be roughly on eight, the second on nine, the fifth on twelve, the ninth on four, etc.) Ideally there are levels or carpeted cubes for each to stand on, with the stargazer occupying the twelve o'clock position being the highest and those occupying the eight and four positions being the lowest, perhaps at ground level.

As the program begins we see the stargazers' backs, but prior to delivering their opening lines—which are spoken with great enthusiasm and reverence—each stargazer in turn will turn around to face the audience. While reciting the verses of Scripture, their eyes and hands are at times lifted heavenward, as dictated by the words being spoken.

VOICE	In the beginning God created the heavens and the earth. And the earth was formless and void, and darkness was over the surface of the deep; and the Spirit of God was moving over the surface of the waters. Then God said, "Let there be light"; and there was light. And God . . . separated the light from the darkness. And God called the light day, and the darkness he called night . . . Then God said, "Let there be lights in the expanse of the heavens to separate the day from the night, and let them be for signs, and for seasons, and for days and years; and let them be for lights in the expanse of the heavens to give light on the earth"; and it was so.
GAZER 1	The heavens declare the glory of God; the skies proclaim the work of his hands. Day after day they pour forth speech; night after night they display knowledge.

GAZER 9	Without a sound or word, silent in the skies, their message reaches out to all the world.
GAZER 5	Lift your eyes and look to the heavens: Who created all these?
GAZER 4	He who made the Pleiades and Orion and changes deep darkness into morning, who also darkens day into night . . . the Lord is his name.
GAZER 6	He who brings out the starry host one by one, and calls them each by name. Because of his great power and mighty strength, not one of them is missing.
GAZER 2	He made the moon for the seasons; the sun knows the place of its setting. Thou dost appoint darkness and it becomes night.
GAZER 7	It is he who made the earth by his power, who established the world by his wisdom; and by his understanding he has stretched out the heavens.
GAZER 8	I am the Lord, and there is no other. I form the light and create darkness . . . With my hands I have . . . commanded all the vast myriads of stars.
GAZER 3	O Lord, our Lord, how majestic is thy name in all the earth, who hast displayed thy splendor above the heavens!*

Upon finishing their lines, each stargazer in turn has frozen in position, looking essentially like a row of mannequins in a variety of artistic poses: some standing, some kneeling, some with eyes gazing toward heaven, a head or two bowed in reverence, some palms uplifted with arms partially or fully extended. The stargazers hold these positions during the music that follows. If at all possible, lights come up only on chorus, only during the music, and only a small amount.

CHORUS	(*hums* Silent Night)

*Verses recited by the Voice and Stargazers:
Gen. 1:1–5, 14–15 NASB   Isa. 40:26 NIV
Psalm 19:1–2 NIV   Psalm 104:19–20 NASB
Psalm 19:3–4 LB   Jer. 10:12 NASB
Isa. 40:20 NIV   Isa. 45:6–7 NIV; 45:12 LB
Amos 5:8 NASB   Psalm 8:1 NASB

	Following the song, the stargazers relax and take neutral positions, possibly sitting or turning their backs to the audience, or just standing with their hands at their sides.
VOICE	The people that walked in darkness have seen a great light: they that dwell in the land of the shadow of death, upon them hath the light shined. . . . For unto us a child is born, unto us a son is given. *(Isaiah 9:2, 6 KJV)*
MUSIC	*(instrumental:* O Little Town of Bethlehem*)*
	Somewhere in the auditorium, perhaps off to one side or in the balcony, a violinist plays. You may wish to make this a duet with piano or simply a piano solo; the important thing is that it is serene and beautiful. After an adequate introduction, the two stargazers closest to the audience read or recite the lines from the Phillips Brooks Christmas carol, avoiding the temptation to employ a singsong rhythm. A brief pause at the end of most lines and a slight hesitation where dashes occur will help create the desired effect. The sense should be that of two angels looking out over the city of Bethlehem on the night of Christ's birth.
GAZER 1	O little town of Bethlehem, How still—we see thee lie. Above thy deep and dreamless sleep The silent stars—go by. Yet in thy dark streets shineth The everlasting Light: The hopes—and fears—of all the years Are met in thee—tonight.
GAZER 9	For Christ is born of Mary, And gathered all above, While mortals sleep, the angels keep Their watch of wondering love. O morning stars, together Proclaim the holy birth! And praises sing—to God the King, And peace to men on earth.
1 AND 9	O holy child of Bethlehem, Descend to us, we pray; Cast out our sin and enter in, Be born in us—today. We hear the Christmas angels The great glad tidings tell; O come to us—abide with us, Our Lord Emmanuel!
CHORUS	*(sings* O Come, O Come, Emmanuel*)*

As the chorus sings, the two speakers become the parents of the Christ child and take nativity-scene positions center stage. Following the song, the second, third, seventh, and eighth stargazers read or recite the Christina Rossetti hymn In the Bleak Midwinter. *You may wish to add some melancholy piano strains beneath the words.*

GAZER 2 — In the bleak midwinter, frosty wind made moan,
Earth stood hard as iron, water like a stone;
Snow had fallen, snow on snow, snow on snow,
In the bleak midwinter, long ago.

GAZER 7 — Our God, heaven cannot hold him, nor earth sustain;
Heaven and earth shall flee away when he comes to reign.
In the bleak midwinter a stableplace sufficed
The Lord God Almighty, Jesus Christ.

GAZER 8 — Angels and archangels may have gathered there,
Cherubim and seraphim thronged the air;
But only his mother, in her maiden bliss,
Worshipped her beloved with a kiss.

GAZER 3 — What can I give him, poor as I am?
If I were a shepherd, I would bring a lamb;
If I were a wise man, I would do my part;
Yet what I can I give him—give him my heart.

VOICE — And there were in the same country
shepherds abiding in the field,
keeping watch over their flock by night.
   (Luke 2:8 KJV)

SOLOIST — (*sings* O Holy Night)

As the song begins, the four stargazers who just spoke move to the front of the stage where they become shepherds in the field: two of them are sitting on the ground, warming themselves by an imaginary fire; another is lying down sleeping; the fourth is standing a few feet away keeping watch. As the song approaches the words "Fall on your knees," the eyes of the standing shepherd suddenly widen in fear. He backs up toward the two sitting shepherds and, without turning his head, nudges one of them. They quickly rise, also slightly horrified; one of them lightly kicks their sleeping cohort, who climbs groggily to his knees at about the same moment the others are falling to their own, in conjunction with the words of the song. As the song continues they rise and make their way to the manger where they take up traditional nativity-scene positions.

VOICE — Behold, there came wise men
from the east to Jerusalem,
saying: Where is he that is
born King of the Jews? For we
have seen his star in the east,
and are come to worship him.
   (Matthew 2:1–2 KJV)

CHORUS	(*sings* Do You Hear What I Hear?)
	(*alternate selection:* One Small Child)

> *The chorus, divided into Group A and Group B, alternates with the three remaining stargazers in reciting the words to the John H. Hopkins Jr. hymn* We Three Kings of Orient Are.

GAZERS	We three kings of Orient are, Bearing gifts we traverse afar—
GAZER 4	Field and fountain—
GAZER 6	Moor and mountain—
GAZER 5	Following yonder star.
GROUP A	Star of wonder—
GROUP B	Star of night—
GROUP A	Star with royal—
GROUP B	Beauty bright—
GROUP A	Westward leading—
GROUP B	Still proceeding—
A AND B	Guide us to thy perfect light.
GAZER 4	Born a king on Bethlehem's plain, Gold I bring to crown him again, King forever, ceasing never Over us all to reign.

> *During the last two lines, he has spread first his right arm, then his left, and now holds them away from his body while the others speak.*

GROUP A	Star of wonder—
GROUP B	Star of night—
GROUP A	Star with royal—
GROUP B	Beauty bright—
GROUP A	Westward leading—
GROUP B	Still proceeding—
A AND B	Guide us to thy perfect light.
GAZER 6	Frankincense to offer have I, Incense owns a deity nigh; Prayer and praising, all men raising, Worship him, God on high.

> *This wise man also, on his final two lines, has spread his arms—first his left, then his right—and now keeps them in that position.*

GROUP A	Star of wonder—
GROUP B	Star of night—
GROUP A	Star with royal—
GROUP B	Beauty bright—
GROUP A	Westward leading—
GROUP B	Still proceeding—
A AND B	Guide us to thy perfect light.

When the final stargazer speaks, it is in a voice and manner that, along with his words, bring the joyful spirit to an abrupt halt. At the end of his second line, in fact, everyone on stage turns and looks at him, shocked at the news he is bringing to such a joyous occasion. His struggle over sharing this painful message is evident from the laborious delivery of his lines.

GAZER 5
Myrrh is mine, its bitter perfume
Breathes a life of gathering gloom;
Sorrowing—sighing—bleeding—dying—
Sealed in a stone-cold tomb.

On his third line, he too has spread his arms, both at once. The other two wise men, whose arms are already outstretched, raise them a bit higher, thus forming with the middle wise man a silhouette of three men hanging on crosses. And because Mary, Joseph, and the shepherds are already looking on from below like a crowd gathered at a crucifixion, the raising of the arms immediately converts the Bethlehem Christmas into a Jerusalem Good Friday. All freeze as a soloist begins wandering through the vignette, singing a cappella or with piano accompaniment.

SOLOIST (sings *I Wonder As I Wander*)

If you have chosen to use adults as stargazers, it would be appropriate to have the woman playing Mary sing the solo. She then could be carrying and looking at the baby in her arms as she sings. At the end of the song she would return to her position in the manger scene. If you are bringing a soloist from offstage, have her—or him—approach Mary during the solo and touch the baby in her arms. Following the song, the soloist can either exit or stand off to one side, gazing at the manger scene. The wise men may lower their arms.

VOICE
Now is the time for judgment on this world;
now the prince of this world will be driven out.
But I, when I am lifted up from the earth,
will draw all men to myself. . . .
I am the light of the world. Whoever
follows me will never walk in darkness,
but will have the light of life.
 (John 12:31–32; 8:12 NIV)

SOLOIST (sings *Sweet Little Jesus Boy*)

PASTOR (Speaks briefly about the real purpose of Christ's coming: our redemption.)

There are two ways to finish this program. Both involve the three wise men coming forward to join the other stargazers. All then advance toward the front of the stage like a group of people approaching with caution. If the song Bethlehem Morning *is used, they are approaching the empty tomb on Easter morning; if the song* We Shall Behold Him *is used, they are witnessing the second coming of Christ. They then react with awe and joy in conjunction with the words of the song as they see the Son of God appear. A mutual point of focus on the back wall or ceiling should be designated so that all will be looking at the same spot. As the song ends, all should kneel humbly with heads bowed. The pastor's remarks prior to this scene should conclude with a lead-in either to the resurrection or second coming, depending on the song chosen.*

SOLOIST (*sings* We Shall Behold Him *by Sandy Patti*)

(*alternate song:* Bethlehem Morning *by Sandy Patti*)

If you feel the need for a closing hymn that the audience can join in on, try the following.

FINALE (*all sing* Christ, Whose Glory Fills the Skies)

(*alternate hymn:* The Light of the World Is Jesus)

Notes to the Director

In putting together your chorus for this program, you may wish to use slightly older children and utilize your youngest children in a sort of pre-program chorus before *Nocturne* begins. The young chorus could sing selections that tie in with the program's nighttime theme, such as *This Little Light of Mine; Give Me Oil in My Lamp; All Night, All Day;* etc.

Choose the stargazers from your oldest, most confident children, or have them played by adults or high-school drama students.

If at all possible, maintain the quiet, artistic nature of this program. Avoid noisy interruptions that will distract from its atmosphere and message.

You Don't Say!

God is speaking . . . He is by His nature
continuously articulate.

A. W. Tozer
The Pursuit of God

Subject

The Word of God.

Setting

Podium, acting area, and chorus.

Summary

1. A mime mails a Christmas card.

2. Two narrators discuss the importance of words.

3. Using no words—only vocal sounds and facial expressions—three young people perform a skit about an "illegal" pre-Christmas gift inspection.

4. Our God is a God who communicates: verses from Scripture illustrate the importance of his word both in creation and in leading his people.

5. God's greatest and final word was his Son, Jesus Christ.

Characters

MIME
NARRATOR A, *female*
NARRATOR B, *male*
SISTER
BROTHER
MOTHER
READERS, *six or more, male and female*
SOLOISTS, *one or two, male or female*
MARY
JOSEPH
SHEPHERDS } *optional*
WISE MEN
CHORUS

The stage needs no special preparation. The normal Christmas decorations will suffice. As the lights go down, the song We Wish You a Merry Christmas *is heard in the background: one or more of your young people performing a piano solo, flute duet, or violin trio, perhaps. A girl dressed in black with red and green trim enters and performs the following brief pantomime:*

Stands center stage, hands on hips, looks around.
Reacts with pleasure as her eyes come to rest on the object of her search: an imaginary Christmas card.
Picks up the card and looks admiringly at the cover.
Smiles and sighs as she reads the words inside.
Crosses to imaginary desk, picks up imaginary pen, and signs card.
Picks up imaginary envelope, inserts card, licks and seals envelope.
Quickly addresses envelope. Thinks a moment to recall those last two digits of the zip code; remembers and writes them down.
Smiles, puts on imaginary jacket, scarf, cap and boots, takes envelope and begins heading toward imaginary front door.
Stops in horror (facing audience), looks at envelope, turns and hurries back to desk.
Looks frantically for something, opening imaginary drawers and tossing imaginary objects every which way.
Relaxes and smiles (facing audience) as she finds the object of her search: an imaginary postage stamp.
Licks stamp and places it on envelope. (To shorten or simplify this scene, eliminate stamp portion.)
Proceeds toward door, opens it, steps through it, closes it, and takes a deep breath as she looks around (facing audience) at what a grand day it is.
Takes a few brisk steps toward an imaginary mailbox.
Opens mailbox, kisses card, and drops it in.
Begins strutting toward exit, smiling.
Stops, a look of concern on her face, steps back to mailbox and reopens it just to make sure the card dropped all the way down. Apparently it has, because a satisfied smile returns to her face as she continues her exit.
Background music ends.

Narrator A and Narrator B enter and stand at the podium off to one side. They may read their lines or speak from memory.

NARRATOR A   Good evening, and welcome to _____. My name is _____ and I'll be one of your announcers tonight. Joining me at the podium is _____.

                           She looks at Narrator B but he is preoccupied. She repeats his first name to get his attention.

NARRATOR B   Oh! Yes—uh, good evening—

NARRATOR A   You seem to be at a loss for words tonight.

NARRATOR B   Sorry. I was just trying to figure out what that opening scene was about.

NARRATOR A   It was about words.

NARRATOR B	Words!
NARRATOR A	Words. You've heard of them?
NARRATOR B	I've not only heard *of* them, I've *heard* them. Many times. And this was definitely not one of those times.
NARRATOR A	What do you mean?
NARRATOR B	No words! She was out here for all that time and she never *said* anything!
NARRATOR A	Of course not! It was a pantomime! Nobody speaks in a pantomime.
NARRATOR B	You mean she wasn't *supposed* to talk?
NARRATOR A	No.
NARRATOR B	Well, why didn't she *say* so?
NARRATOR A	*(sends him a "give-me-a-break" look)*
NARRATOR B	I know, I know. She wasn't allowed. *(pause)* So what was the point of it anyway?
NARRATOR A	Words.
NARRATOR B	Words?
NARRATOR A	Words.
NARRATOR B	There *were* no words.
NARRATOR A	That was the point.
NARRATOR B	Oh. *(sarcastic)* The point of the whole thing was words, of which there were none. *(shrugs)* Makes sense to *me*.
NARRATOR A	It makes perfect sense. We're emphasizing the significance of words by demonstrating their absence. I mean, did you ever stop and think about how *valuable* words are?
NARRATOR B	*(having fun)* I could talk to you all day on that subject.
NARRATOR A	Or about how dependent we are on them?
NARRATOR B	I'd like to have a word with you about that sometime.
NARRATOR A	Or where we would be without them?
NARRATOR B	*(shrugs)* I'm speechless.
NARRATOR A	Imagine for a moment what it would be like if we had to get by without any words at all.
	Lights come up on stage. Sister enters and sits down to read. After a few seconds Brother enters cautiously, checking first to see if coast is clear. He tiptoes toward a pile of gift-wrapped packages underneath a Christmas tree or on a table. Sister has seen him approaching and is observing him unnoticed.
SISTER	*(clearing her throat as a warning)* Heh-heh-hemm!
BROTHER	*(spins around, startled; puts hand over his heart to indicate she scared him)* Whew! *(finger to lips)* Shhhh!

He goes to gifts and picks out a large box, brings it forward and sets it down, then begins opening it, being very careful not to leave any evidence. Every few seconds he looks up again, making sure no one is coming. Sister rises to look over his shoulder.

SISTER: *(singsongy; disapproving)* Uh-uh-uuhhh.

BROTHER: *(turns, growls at her)* Grrrr. *(makes a fist)*

SISTER: *(over her shoulder as she returns to chair; unintimidated)* Ayyyy.

BROTHER: *(delighted with contents of package)* Mmmmm.

Sister, observing, rolls her eyes. Brother is so caught up in examining the gift that he fails to notice Mother enter silently and stand watching, her arms crossed. Sister notices and smiles.

SISTER: *(whistles delightedly)*

BROTHER: *(turning to look)* Hmmm? *(sees Mother)* Uh-oh.

Mother tilts her head and gives him a slightly-disapproving-but-tempered-by-the-Christmas-spirit look, then shakes her head and sighs. He cringes and closes the gift back up, then returns it to the pile.

SISTER: *(during above action: hums Taps)*

BROTHER: *(looks meekly at Mother, draws index finger across his neck like he's going to lose his neck, makes cutting sound.)*

MOTHER: Uh-huh. *(motions with index finger that he's to come with her; shakes her head, clucks her tongue as she exits)*

SISTER: *(singing to melody that baseball fans use to taunt opposing pitchers being pulled from lineup)* Nah nah nah nah, nah nah nah nah, hey hey—

BROTHER: *(spins around, glares at her, hands on hips)*

SISTER: *(instead of singing the word good-bye, waves coyly, trying to get his goat)*

BROTHER: *(his goat got, gives a frustrated sigh and exits)*

SISTER: *(as she thrusts her fist forward; exuberant)* Yesss!

Sister puts hand to her mouth, realizing she used a word. Runs off as lights fade on stage and come up again on podium.

NARRATOR B: Well, I got the point this time.

NARRATOR A: Okay, what is it?

NARRATOR B: Make sure the coast is clear if you're going to be doing something you're not supposed to be doing.

NARRATOR A: That's not the point at all.

NARRATOR B: Then what?

NARRATOR A: That even without words, people are always finding ways to communicate. That's the way God made us: We're creatures of communication. And because we are made in the image of God, it's easy to understand that God, too, is interested in communication. Of course, that's obvious from the Bible.

Destination Bethlehem

NARRATOR B	Yes, it's *full* of words.
NARRATOR A	Of course. It wouldn't be a *book* without *words*.
NARRATOR B	Wouldn't be worth *reading* without words, that's for sure.
NARRATOR A	*(amused)* No, I suppose not.
NARRATOR B	I mean, just a couple of covers. That's all there'd be.
NARRATOR A	Yes.
NARRATOR B	Front and back.
NARRATOR A	Okay. *(still amused but wants to get back to the program)*
NARRATOR B	Do you think it would still be inspired?
NARRATOR A	*(rolls her eyes and sighs)*
NARRATOR B	If it was just a cover, I mean. We couldn't call it the Word of God anymore, could we. *(beat)* Not if there weren't any words.
NARRATOR A	The point is—
NARRATOR B	Oh yes, the point.
NARRATOR A	The point is, our God is a God who speaks. It began all the way back at creation.
NARRATOR B	You don't say.
NARRATOR A	Yes! He spoke everything into existence.

    Lights come up on six readers who share verses from the first chapter of Genesis, NIV translation.

READER 1	And God said, "Let there be light."
READERS	And there was light.
READER 2	And God said, "Let the water under the sky be gathered to one place, and let dry ground appear."
READERS	And it was so.
READER 3	Then God said, "Let the land produce vegetation."
READERS	And it was so.
READER 4	And God said, "Let there be lights in the expanse of the sky to separate the day from the night, and let them serve as signs to mark seasons and days and years."
READERS	And it was so.
READER 5	And God said, "Let the water teem with living creatures, and let birds fly above the earth . . ." And God said, "Let the land produce living creatures according to their kinds."

You Don't Say!

READERS	And it was so.
READER 6	*(reverently)* Then God said, "Let us make man in our image."
READERS	*(softly)* Ahhh.

Lights fade on readers and come up on podium.

NARRATOR A	But God spoke in another way also.
NARRATOR B	How's that?
NARRATOR A	Through his prophets.
NARRATOR B	Oh, yes. Everyone profits from listening to the words of the prophets.
NARRATOR A	You can pun all you like, but it's true: When God had things he wanted to share with his people, he spoke through men who would pass that word on to those who needed to hear it.
NARRATOR B	Men like . . . Jeremiah?
NARRATOR A	Yes.
NARRATOR B	And uh . . . Isaiah?
NARRATOR A	Yes.
NARRATOR B	And . . . Ezekiel?
NARRATOR A	Uh-huh.
NARRATOR B	Daniel?
NARRATOR A	Right.
NARRATOR B	Obadiah, Zephaniah, and Zechariah?
NARRATOR A	*(doing a double take)* Yes!
NARRATOR B	Amos and Micah and Malachi?
NARRATOR A	*(impressed)* Precisely.
NARRATOR B	Hosea, Habakkuk, and Haggai?
NARRATOR A	Wow.
NARRATOR B	Shakespeare and Chaucer?
NARRATOR A	*(beat)* What?
NARRATOR B	Just checking.
NARRATOR A	Boy, you sure do know your Bible.
NARRATOR B	Every word of it.
NARRATOR A	Cute.
NARRATOR B	But tell me. You're talking about people through whom God spoke.
NARRATOR A	Yes.

Destination Bethlehem

NARRATOR B	What about Moses? And King David and King Solomon? Weren't they also men who shared the words of God?
NARRATOR A	Absolutely. They weren't prophets in the same way that *Jonah* was, for instance, but as leaders of God's people they spoke and wrote God's words for the benefit of all of us.

Lights come up on readers who share verses from the LB translation of Psalm 119:89, 96–98, 101–103, 105–106; NASB translation of Proverbs 4:20–22; and LB translation of Isaiah 40:6–8.

READER 1	The Psalmist writes—
READER 2	Forever, O Lord, your Word stands firm in heaven.
READER 3	Nothing is perfect except your words. Oh, how I love them. I think about them all day long. They make me wiser than my enemies, because they are my constant guide.
READER 4	I have refused to walk the paths of evil for I will remain obedient to your Word. No, I haven't turned away from what you taught me; your words are sweeter than honey.
READER 5	Your words are a flashlight to light the path ahead of me, and keep me from stumbling. I've said it once and I'll say it again and again: I will obey these wonderful laws of yours.
READER 6	And King Solomon says:
READER 1	My son, give attention to my words.
READER 2	Incline your ear to my sayings.
READER 3	Do not let them depart from your sight.
READER 4	Keep them in the midst of your heart.
READER 5	For they are life to those who find them.
READER 6	And health to all their whole body.
READER 1	Listen to these words of the prophet Isaiah!
READER 2	The voice says, "Shout!"
READER 3	"What shall I shout?" I asked.
READER 4	"Shout that man is like the grass that dies away, and all his beauty fades like dying flowers.
READER 5	The grass withers, the flower fades beneath the breath of God.
READER 6	And so it is with fragile man.

	The grass withers, the flowers fade—
READERS	*(almost a whisper)* But the Word of our God shall stand forever."

Lights fade on readers, come up on podium.

NARRATOR A	So—now we have two ways that God has spoken.
NARRATOR B	Yes. By the Word of his mouth he *created* the world, and then he entrusted prophets and leaders to pass on his words to the *people* of that world.
NARRATOR A	Collected in a book, these are known as the Word of God—the Bible.
NARRATOR B	The end.
NARRATOR A	*Huh?*
NARRATOR B	We're not finished?
NARRATOR A	Of course not! This is a Christmas program!
NARRATOR B	Oh—yeah. And we haven't even had—
NARRATOR A	Right. *(back to program)* Because there's a *third* way that God has spoken.
NARRATOR B	A third word?
NARRATOR A	Yes—a third word: the Word known as Jesus Christ.

Lights fade on podium, come up on six readers who will share from NIV translation of John 1:1–5, 10–12, 14; and Hebrews 1:1–3.

READER 1	In the beginning was the Word, and the Word was with God, and the Word was God.
READER 2	He was with God in the beginning.
READER 3	Through him all things were made; without him nothing was made that has been made.
READER 4	In him was life, and that life was the light of men.
READER 5	The light shines in the darkness, but the darkness has not understood it.
READER 6	He was in the world, and though the world was made through him, the world did not recognize him.
READER 1	He came to that which was his own, but his own did not receive him.
READER 2	Yet to all who received him, to those who believed in his name, he gave the right to become children of God.
READER 3	The Word became flesh and lived for a while among us.

Destination Bethlehem

READER 4	In the past God spoke to our forefathers through the prophets at many times and in various ways.
READER 5	But in these last days he has spoken to us by his Son . . . through whom he made the universe.
READER 6	The Son is the radiance of God's glory and the exact representation of his being, sustaining all things by his powerful word.

Lights fade and return again to podium.

NARRATOR B	Need we say more?
NARRATOR A	*(shaking her head)* God said it all—when he sent the Word to us at Christmas.
SOLOIST	*(sings* The Final Word *by Michael Card)*

During the solo, Mary and Joseph enter and form the beginnings of a manger scene. If you wish, they can wait until a later song, or you may wish to do the program with songs only and no manger scene, or even to end the program with this solo.

CHORUS	*(sings* Do You Hear What I Hear?*)*

Shepherds and wise men may be added to the manger scene during this song, then all remain in place during the following song.

CHORUS	*(sings* What Child Is This?*)*
PASTOR	My final word to you tonight is this: God is speaking to you, through his creation, through his written Word—the Bible, and through his living Word—Jesus Christ. Let us tell him, with *our* words, that we wish to be his people, to know his forgiveness, to know him. *(Leads the audience in prayer.)*
SOLOIST	*(sings* The Word *by Michael Card)*
CHORUS	*(sings* Feliz Navidad*)*
FINALE	*(audience sings* I Know Not Why God's Wondrous Grace*)*

Notes to the Director

The six readers may be the same six people throughout, or you may wish to use more of your young people and bring in a new group for each segment. Another alternative is to have the Isaiah, Solomon, and psalmist lines read by three boys dressed in appropriate costumes. The lines then would not be divided up among several readers.

Songs that a young choir might perform prior to the program:
Wonderful Words of Life
The B-I-B-L-E
Jesus Loves Me
Love Letters of Christmas
There Is Power in the Name of Jesus
He's Got the Whole World in His Hands

Appendix: Music Sources

The following is a list of the songs suggested in this book. The codes accompanying the titles indicate sources for obtaining background tapes and/or sheet music. A key to the codes follows the list.

All Night, All Day: KP

Angels We Have Heard on High: BH, CC, KC, MM, MS, ST, WS

Assurance March: KP

As with Gladness Men of Old: In many hymnals

Away in a Manger: BH, CC, DT, KC, MM, MS, ST

Bethlehem Morning: BH, MM, WC, WS

B-I-B-L-E, The: FS, KP

Bring a Torch, Jeanette, Isabella: KC

Celebrate the Season: KC

Christ, Whose Glory Fills the Skies: In many hymnals

Do You Hear What I Hear?: MM, ST

Feliz Navidad: KC

Final Word, The: SPW, ST

First Noel, The: CC, DT, KC, MM, MS, ST, WC, WS

Frosty the Snowman: MM

Give Me Oil in My Lamp: KP

Go Tell It on the Mountain: BH, BT, CC, KC, KP, MM

Here We Come A-Caroling: CC, KC

He's Got the Whole World in His Hands: KP

I Know Not Why God's Wondrous Grace: In many hymnals

Immanuel: SPW. This song is available either in sheet music as listed or in a combination track (along with "Celebrate the Child") from Sparrow (Choral Trax). This would be a fitting number for the end of "Buster Come Back" because the song repeats the words "No more wandering in the night." The song will fit into any Christmas program as it deals with the birth of Jesus. (See SP for ordering information.)

Into My Heart: KP

I Wonder as I Wander: MM, WS

Jesus Loves Even Me: FS, KP

Jesus Loves Me: FS, KP

Joy in the Journey: SPW, ST

Joy to the World: CC, DT, KC MM, MS

Light of the World Is Jesus, The: In many hymnals

Love Letters of Christmas: KC

Noah (Arky, Arky): FS, KP

O Come, All Ye Faithful: BH, CC, DT, KC, MM, MS, ST

O Come, Little Children: CC, KC

O Come, O Come Emmanuel: CC, ST, WS

O Holy Night: BH, BT, CC, DT, MM, ST, WS

O Little Town of Bethlehem: CC, DT, MM, MS

One Small Child: WC, WS

Only a Boy Named David: KP

Over the River and through the Woods: KC

Ring the Bells: KC

Rise, Come and See the King: KC

Silent Night: BT, CC, DT, KC, MM, MS, WS

Somewhere It's Snowing: PM

Sweet Little Jesus Boy: BH, BT, MM

There Is Power in the Name of Jesus: KP

This Little Light of Mine: FS, KP

Turn Your Heart toward Home: SS

Virgin Mary Had a Baby Boy, The: KC, MM

We Shall Behold Him: BSM, WS

We Three Kings of Orient Are: CC, DT

We Wish You a Merry Christmas: CC, KC, MM, WC

What Child Is This: BH, CC, DT, MM, ST

While Shepherds Watched Their Flocks: CC, KC, MS

With a Star That Bright: KC
Wonderful Words of Life: WS
Word, The: SPF, SPW, ST

Key

BH Benson HiLo Trax are available from Benson Music Group, 365 Great Circle Road, Nashville, TN 37228, 1-800-444-4012.

BSM Benson Sheet Music (see BH for ordering information)

BT Benson Master Trax (see BH for ordering information)

CC *Carols of Christmas* (Music Edition). Caroling songbook available from Augsburg Publishing House, Minneapolis, Minnesota, or from Malecki Music, Inc. (see MM for ordering information)

DT Dove Tracks are available from Nashville Sound Plus You, Inc., P.O. Box 101600, Nashville, TN 37210, 1-800-824-6167.

FS *The First Sunday Sing-A-Long: 34 Great Sunday School Songs of Yesterday and Today* by the Maranatha! Kids (a split-track recording providing background accompaniment for performance). Available from Benson Music Group (see BH for ordering information).

KC *Kids Sing Christmas: 31 Kids' Christmas Favorites Sung by Kids* (a split-track recording providing background accompaniment for performance). Tape or songbook available from Brentwood Music, Inc., 316 Southgate Court, Brentwood, TN 37027, 1-800-333-9000.

KP *Kids Sing Praise: 43 Praise, Scripture and Sing-along Fun Songs* (a split-track recording providing background accompaniment for performance). Tape or songbook available from Brentwood Music (see KC for ordering information).

MM A wide variety of sheet music, songbooks, choral arrangements, and accompaniment tracks are available from Malecki Music, Inc., located in Grand Rapids, Michigan (1-800-253-9692), Council Bluffs, Iowa (1-800-831-4197), Spokane, Washington (1-800-541-2001), and Long Beach, California (1-800-858-7664).

MS *Maranatha! Music Presents Sing-A-Long Christmas for Kids: 15 Kids' Choir Arrangements,* available from the Benson Company (see BH for ordering information).

PM Paragon Music Corp/Sound III has two versions of *Somewhere It's Snowing*. Available from: Christian World Incorporated, Oklahoma City, OK 73107, 1-800-654-6760.

SP Sparrow Print Music is available from: Sparrow Distribution, 101 Winners Circle, Brentwood, TN 37027, 1-800-877-4443, (FAX 615-371-6980).

SPF Available from Sparrow Print Music under the book title *Find Us Faithful* (see SP for ordering information).

SPW Available from Sparrow Print Music under the book title *The Final Word* (see SP for ordering information).

SS Available from Star Song Communications, 306 Sundown Trail, Williamsville, NY 14221, 1-800-TELSONG.

ST Sparrow Solo Trax are available from Sparrow Distribution (see SP for ordering information).

WC Word ChoralTrax are available from Word, Inc., P.O. Box 2518, Waco, TX 76702, 1-800-933-9673.

WS Accompaniment tracks from the Word Studio Series are available from Word, Inc. (see WC for ordering information).